W9-BYF-925

DISCARDED

Stan Getz Library
Berklee College of Music

"It had long since come to my attention that people of
accomplishment rarely sat back and let things happen to them.
They went out and happened to things." - - **Leonardo da Vinci**

DISCARDED

Communicating with the Future

How re-engineering intentions will alter the master code of our future

By Futurist Thomas Frey

Louisville, Colorado, USA

DAVINCI INSTITUTE PRESS

Copyright © 2011 by Thomas J. Frey. All rights reserved. Printed in the United States of America. Except as permitted under the United States Copyright Act of 1976, no part of this publication may be reproduced or distributed in any form or by any means, or stored in a database or retrieval system, without prior written permission from the DaVinci Institute.

LIBRARY OF CONGRESS CATALOGING-IN-PUBLICATION DATA

Frey, Thomas J.
  Communicating with the Future: How re-engineering intentions will alter the master code of our future / by Thomas J. Frey

Preface

Our journey into the future is never ending. It begins at the moment of our birth and continues forever.

Until now, we have viewed ourselves as "victims" of the future, having to accept whatever life dishes out for us. However, it doesn't have to be that way.

This book is based on breakthrough tools and techniques that you can use to gain some measure of control over the future.

Unlike books of mysticism that require a leap of faith, "Communicating with the Future" is based on a well-established cutting edge business practices. And yes, this is a proven methodology for controlling the future... well, parts of it.

As I always like to say, "Why bother predicting the future when you can control it?"

Acknowledgements

The people who you surround yourself with have a huge impact on where you end up in life, and I'm honored to be surrounded by some of the best and brightest in the world.

The DaVinci Institute has attracted a considerable following since 1997 when it was first formed, and I now find myself in the company of remarkable people leading remarkable lives.

To the Senior Fellows who serve as the elite brain trust for the Institute, I offer my sincerest thanks and appreciation.

To those of you who have participated in the Futurist Mastermind Groups and the Mad Scientist Club, I will forever be indebted to your brilliance.

To our newly formed Council of Luminaries who serve as the mentor network for our coworking companies at The Vault, you serve as an inspiration to all of us.

To the members of the DaVinci Institute, we owe you a debt of gratitude. You are the ones who have made the Institute what it is today.

To our staff at the Institute – my assistant and all-around handle everything person Jan Wagner, Steve Maltz, Darby Frey, Mike Morgan, Andrew Frey, David Baur-Ray, and all of our volunteers – you make the work we do seem easy and fun. To you my sincerest thanks and appreciation.

To Rick and Nichole Dowlearn who helped make this book a reality; to Cara Russell who worked as the editor; and Mike Hamers from Lightspeed Commercial Art who created the cover design, a special thank you.

To my kids, Darby, Shandra, Kyler, Nicole, Jessica, and Bryan who love listening to my half-baked theories, challenge my thinking, and constantly keep me on task, I couldn't do this work without you. You serve as the daily inspiration for everything that I do.

And most importantly, to my wife Deb who serves as Vice President of the DaVinci Institute, but also my right-hand person, booking agent, sounding board for crazy ideas, and all-around organizer of the unorganized, none of this would have happened without you.

What people are saying…

Here are a few of the comments we've been getting on "Communicating with the Future."

"Thomas Frey offers a clear-eyed tour of skills that can make change much less fearful. Change can be examined, understood, and even turned into opportunity." - - International best selling science fiction writer **David Brin**, author of *The Postman*

"An ambitious and optimistic glimpse into the world of tomorrow by a wise and diligent student of the future." – - Former Colorado Governor, **Richard Lamm**

"The most readable and far-reaching futuring process to date" - - **Dennis Bushnell**, Chief Scientist, NASA

"Thought provoking and on-target. A compelling new strategy for leading edge innovation. True innovation happens when we are able to anticipate the needs of consumers BEFORE they know they need it. This book provides the thought provoking issues that face all innovators and delivers the meaningful lessons to increase the likelihood of success." - - **Louis Foreman** – CEO of EdisonNation and Publisher of *Inventor Digest Magazine*

"I believe we all have been communicating with the future, but I now have a deeper understanding. Brilliant!" - - **Thomas Franklin**, Partner, Kilpatrick Townsend

"…shows how we can become completely proactive about many aspects of our lives!" - - **Cate Lawrence**, founder of Lawrence Research

"…an essential tool for your toolbox." - - **Karl Dakin**, Executive Director of the Sullivan Chair for Free Enterprise at Regis University

"If we are simultaneously the clay and the sculptor of the future as Thomas suggests, then *Communicating with the Future* is the craftsman's guide for molding our destiny." - - **Michael Cushman**, CEO of the Keychange Institute

"*Communicating with the Future* is a relief, an inspiration and a valuable tool for all of us who toil in these interesting times." - - **Peter Vandevanter**, Founder of the Personalize MEdia Conference."

"This book gives me an 'unfair advantage' over the competition because I can now influence outcomes and invent the future. So simple yet so powerful!" - - **Michael W. Miller**, VP, COO Engage Communication Group

"An insightful, thought-provoking fresh look at how our world marches forward and how we can become masters of our own future." - - **Bert Vermeulen**, Senior Fellow at the DaVinci Institute

"Thomas is a highly intelligent deep thinker but he is also down to earth with a good sense of humor that shines through in his writing. I think this book should become a college course for future leaders." - - **Steve Baker**, Author of *Pushing Water Uphill with a Rake*

Contents

1

Looking Forward into the Future

"Much like walking through a dark forest with a flashlight, the future comes into focus only a short distance in front of us. So how do we create a brighter flashlight?"

We are a very backward-looking society.

We're very backward-looking in that we've all personally experienced the past. As we look around, we see evidence of the past all around us. The past is very knowable, yet we will spend the rest of our lives in the future.

My job as a futurist is to help turn people around and give them some idea of what the future holds.

So, what images come to mind when you think about the future?

If you're like most people, you have some persistent vision of the future that keeps replaying in your head. Perhaps it's an image of riding on a hover board, traveling in a flying car or stopping at a space hotel.

Many of these visions have been planted in your head through the movies you watch or the magazines and books that you read.

More important than how they were created is the question, "Who owns these visions?"

I'm not talking about the intellectual property rights associated with these images. Rather, I am asking who is it that cares enough about these particular visions to want to take an ownership stake in their creation and bring them to fruition?

In the vast majority of all cases, the answer is simply, "no one."

In the years ahead, the speed of business will continue to accelerate, and executive teams will quickly learn that simply planning for the future is no longer good enough. In order for them to better control their own destiny, they will need to take an ownership stake in the creation of the future. That's why this book is so important.

Until now, the science of the future has been a murky science. The tools are primitive, reputations are often suspect, and the unknowns continue to dominate the path ahead.

Scenario planning, trend analysis, demographic shifts, and cyclical patterns are all tiny Braille bumps on the looming mosaic that constitutes our future, and some of our best and brightest continue to be confounded when it comes to predicting the future because they lack the tools to communicate with the future.

THE CRYSTAL BALL

As a futurist, I often get asked, "Do you have a crystal ball?"

And the answer is "yes." I do.

Looking forward into the Future

A few weeks back, my wife, Deb, asked me to take the crystal ball to the office because it was just collecting dust at home. So I did.

But before going to the office, I had a meeting in Denver and I was riding down the interstate with my crystal ball on the seat next to me — sparkling across some magazines and papers.

I was no more than five miles down the road when I smelled smoke.

I looked over and saw that my crystal ball had ignited a fire next to me. With the sun shining in, the crystal ball served as a giant lens and caught the paper on fire as any boy scout could have predicted, although I hadn't.

Luckily, I was able to put out the flames with no real damage to my car and was quick to cover up the crystal ball lest there be another incident.

But for the rest of the trip, I kept having this reoccurring vision in my head: a newspaper headline on the front page reads:

"Futurist Killed by His Own Crystal Ball
...and He Didn't See It Coming!"

Obviously, I am not suggesting the crystal ball as a tool for foreseeing the future. In fact, I found it to be a hazard. However there are some valuable and less mystic tools that can be used to communicate with the future.

Furthermore, what if we step beyond simply predicting the future and instead work on controlling it?

To illustrate my point, allow me to look backwards for just a moment.

Communicating with the Future

In 1972, I was a young engineering student at South Dakota State University in Brookings. One of the first courses I was required to take was a short course on slide rules. For those of you who don't know what a slide rule is, it is a calculation tool. First came the abacus, then came the slide rule, and then came the calculator.

This was a time when the real "cool geeks" on campus walked around proudly displaying their black carrying case for their slide rule that was attached to their belt — "brainiacs" on parade – a way of telling the world how smart they were.

Early calculators were first showing their face around 1970, but in 1972 they were still pretty expensive. I remember arguing with my teacher about whether or not the slide rule course was necessary and his response was that "all engineers need to know how to run the slide rule." At the time, I thought it was tough to argue with that logic.

But of course his thinking was wrong. Even though I took the course and passed it with flying colors, I've never even once used a slide rule in doing engineering work. Engineers at Hewlett-Packard and Texas Instruments who were working on next-generation calculators at the time would have laughed at my teacher's assertion that slide rules were always going to be the centerpiece of the engineer's tool chest.

Clearly this period of time was the end of an era. It was the end of the slide rule era and the beginning of the calculator era.

As a society, we haven't seen the end of too many eras, but we are on the verge of experiencing many things disappearing in the near future. Most won't be as cleanly defined as the slide rule being replaced by the calculator. Often times, the soon-to-be-obsolete technology will be replaced by two or three other technologies.

As I sketched out the simple diagram showing the end of one era and the beginning of another, the point where the two eras overlapped caught my attention. This period of time was important to isolate because of the extreme dynamics happening there. It also occurred to me that we didn't have a name for this intersection of technology, this collision of business forces.

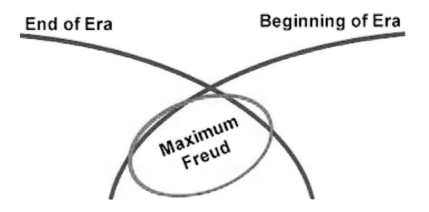

So I came up with the name "Maximum Freud." Yes, it's a rather wacky name, but it makes sense.

As technologies approach Maximum Freud, this is the period when industry players have to spend lots of time on the Freudian Couch to understand what's going on. This is a period of extreme chaos, and also a period of extreme opportunity. But here's the most important part: All technologies end.

Every technology that we use today will someday go away, and it will be replaced by something else. Every technology will approach its own period of Maximum Freud. So from the standpoint of making bold predictions, the imminent demise of many of our technologies is a certainty.

Here are just a few examples of technologies that are currently approaching Maximum Freud:

- CHECKING INDUSTRY

  It is already in decline. The demise of the handwritten check is drawing near. Within ten years the appearance of a paper check will be quite rare.

- FAX MACHINE

  Museum curators are already dusting off a spot for this former staple of the business world. Already in its twilight, the remaining days of the fax machine are numbered.

- TRADITIONAL AM-FM RADIO

  With commercial-free satellite radio making major inroads, the success of iPods and other MP3 players, and Internet radio gaining ground, traditional radio has been losing ground quickly.

- BROADCAST TELEVISION

  Internet TV is gaining ground. Pay-per-view options along with Redbox DVD rentals, Roku, and services like Netflix are all causing the traditional broadcast TV market to dwindle.

- WIRES

  As we move further into the wireless age, more and more of our wired infrastructure will begin to disappear. First the cable television lines, then the telephone wires, and eventually the power lines.

As you can see, the Maximum Freud concept can be a valuable tool in determining which of the business and home products you use today will be gone tomorrow. We live in a very fluid, changing world; each step we take towards the future will enable us to experience life in a new and different way.

In other words, the future will happen with or without us, whether or not we decide to participate. It follows then, that if your next project is not aligned with the problems, needs and desires of the future — the future will kill it!

So how is the future created?

It is created in the minds of the people around us.

PLANTING THE VISION SEED

Our visions drive us forward. Great visions have a way of infecting nearly everyone they touch. As ideas flow into a crowded room, they create wants, needs and desires, and these, in turn, create markets. Businesses have become very good at spotting the unmet desires of people, by developing products that fulfill them.

This cyclical force of meeting market demand creates entirely new economies. And it all starts with the vision.

A vision can be a very powerful tool.

Visions come in many forms. Sometimes a vision is nothing more than a fleeting thought in the middle of the day, other times a vision spontaneously develops into elaborate plans demanding a person's full attention for days on end.

The more detailed a vision is, the more doable it becomes. A vision comprised of only a few words on a page cannot possibly compare on the likelihood-of-things-happening-scale to a detailed vision that comes with a complete business plan, pro formas, schematic diagrams, parts lists and animated video.

The vision is only the beginning.

Communicating with the Future

A great vision begins more as an art form than a science, later adding details, attributes and emotional commitment as it progresses along on the path to realism.

There are many visions for new technologies, some a few years off, others a few decades away, and still others that will never happen. But most visions are like tiny seedlings; they are fighting for the nutrients they gain from mindshare as they spring to life.

It's quite common, however, for industry politics to come into play, and many of these seedling-like visions get destroyed prematurely. For some, a new way of doing things can be a threat to another person's research, and a preemptive strike is considered necessary as a way of protecting a few square miles of scientific turf.

It's interesting to note, however, that industry observers are becoming far better at looking toward the future. For some, a preemptive strike on the credibility of one form of research can also be viewed as a signal to pay attention to the situation. It also has a way of driving key pieces of research underground, to emerge later as a more durable body of work.

In other words, we've learned from the past.

LESSONS FROM THE ANCIENT WORLD

During the time of the ancient Greek civilization, several mathematicians became famous for their work. People like Archimedes, Pythagoras, Euclid, Hipparchus, Posidonius and Ptolemy all brought new elements of thinking to society, furthering the field of math — building on the earlier work of Babylonian and Egyptian mathematicians.

Looking forward into the Future

A few generations later, the Romans became the dominant society on Earth, but mathematicians were notably absent from this society. Rest assured, the scholarly members of Roman society came from a good gene pool and they were every bit as gifted and talented as the Greeks.

But Roman society was being held hostage by its own systems. The primary culprit for the lack of Roman mathematicians was their numbering system — Roman numerals.

While it is easy for us today to look at Roman numerals and say that it was a pretty stupid numbering system, it was just one of many inferior numbering systems in ancient times.

But the feature that made Roman numerals so inferior was the fact that it wasn't a positional numbering system. There are no placeholders for the ones, tens, hundreds, thousands, etc. As a result, each number is an equation, and this extra layer of complexity prevented the people from doing any higher math.

Roman numerals were a system problem, and a huge one at that. They prevented an entire civilization from furthering the field of math and science.

Roman society was so immersed in their numbering system that they had no clue that it was preventing them from doing even rudimentary math such as adding a column of numbers or simple multiplication or division — a feat handled by the abacus. It also prevented them from creating sophisticated banking and accounting systems and restricted academia from moving forward in areas of science, astronomy and medicine.

Ratchet forward to today.

We live in a society where virtually everything is different from the days of the Roman Empire. But what seems so counterintuitive is that we are even more dependent today on our systems than the Romans ever were.

Most of these systems we take for granted — our systems for weights, measurement, accounting, banking, procurement, traffic and food. With each of these systems, we are much like the Romans, immersed in the use of them to a point where we seldom step back and question the reasoning and logic behind them.

Our systems govern virtually every aspect of our lives. They determine how we live and where we live, what we eat and where we work, where and when we travel, how much money we will make, the job we do, the friends we have, who we marry, and even how long we will live.

But much like fish not understanding what water is — we seldom step back to understand the context of our existence.

So what systems do we employ today that are the equivalent of Roman numerals that are preventing us from doing great things?

This simple question is very revealing.

It draws attention to the Pandora 's box full of friction points, inefficiencies and flow restrictors that we contend with every day. Our systems are what govern the flow of commerce and our effectiveness as members of society. They create much of the stress we face on a daily basis.

After studying American systems and applying this "equivalency to Roman numerals" test, it is easy to conclude that we are operating at somewhere between 5-10 percent efficiency, maybe less.

So what are some examples of restrictive systems that are preventing us from doing great things? Here are just a few examples:

- **Stifling Income Tax System** - The income tax system is currently the mother of all boat anchors, slowing commerce and the pace of business to a crawl. Currently somewhere in the neighborhood of 64,000 pages in length, the U.S. tax code that we use today will stand as a shining example throughout history as one of the world's most incomprehensible systems.

- **Half-Implemented Metric System** - America is well known for its half-implemented metric system in which people are purchasing cars with 3.2-liter engines and filling them with quarts of oil. Several disasters have been attributed to the engineering complexities involved in converting between English and Metric systems.

- **Stagnant Keyboards** - Stemming from the days of mechanical typewriters with type bars that were easy to jam, we still use keyboards that were designed to slow the speed of typists by placing the most frequently used keys randomly across the face of the keyboard. But keyboards in any configuration are an extremely inefficient way to transfer knowledge from one person to another.

- **Overloaded Laws** - We now have more laws on the books in the United States than any country at any time in history. There aren't even any good estimates as to the number of laws we   have. With each city, county, state, federal agency and taxing district able to issue their own regulations, mandates, ordinances and laws, we have created a legal snake pit of intertwined and overlapping rules that we are expected to live by.

Lest you think the U.S. is the only country with system problems, consider some of the major issues plaguing other countries:

- **Chinese Alphabet** - The number of Chinese characters contained in the Kangxi dictionary is approximately 47,035, although a large number of these are rarely used variants accumulated over time. Studies carried out in China have shown that full literacy requires knowledge of between three and four thousand characters.

- **Indian Languages** - The country of India has a diverse number of languages spoken by various groups of people. At least 800 different languages and around 2,000 dialects have been identified. The constitution of India has mandated that Hindi and English be the official two languages of communication for the central government. However, each of India's state governments is free to name their own official language.

- **Japanese Currencies** - Japan has become the global laboratory for experimental and complementary currencies with the number of officially sanctioned currencies now exceeding 600.

Much like the rest of the world, we are a long way from optimizing the systems that govern our lives. Inefficiencies have become the status quo with most people resigned to "leave well enough alone."

But the freedom that we value so highly in the United States is only a fraction of what it could be. Our ability to confront and deal with some of the big problems ahead is highly dependent upon our ability to seriously reinvent society, one system at a time.

And how do you do that? By building your vision.

Step 1: Build Your Vision

"Until now, ours has been a dance with the ordinary."

People make decisions today based on their interpretation of what the future holds.

The future *creates* the present.

So, if we change people's visions of the future, we change the way they make decisions. How do we change people's visions of the future? By accomplishing what I call "building a vision."

Let's take another look backwards.

I love Leonardo DaVinci, and as a consequence, the organization that I founded to foster new inventions and fuel higher thought is named *The DaVinci Institute*.

Leonardo was an artist. For this reason, his name immediately conjures the Mona Lisa, the Last Supper, and Vitruvian Man. But aside from his virtuosity in the realm of art, his intense intellectual curiosity led him to explore the nascent worlds of biological sciences and engineering.

Personally, however, I connect with DaVinci's dream of flight. Leonardo DaVinci dedicated over 500 drawings and 35,000 words to the concept of flying, centuries before hot air balloons and the Wright Brothers. These visions of the future were the inspiration of thousands who attempted to build flying machines and fulfill the dream.

Most people believe the future to be a random set of unpredictable occurrences. However, most aspects of the future can be predicted with a high degree of probability.

For example, we can predict with high probability that the:

- Earth will travel around the sun in the same orbit 50 years from now

- Laws of gravity will still be in effect 100 years from now

- People of Earth will still need to communicate 100 years from now

- Seasons of spring, summer, fall and winter will still occur 50 years from now

On a smaller scale, we can predict with high probability that if we:

- Plant seeds they will grow into plants

- Plan a birthday party for two weeks from now it will likely happen

- Knead yeast into dough it will rise within a few hours

Step 1: Build Your Vision

Most of our future is being formed upon the foundation of stable slow-changing elements that are highly predictable. After all, the universe, as we understand it, operates according to a number of laws.

The magicians in the ancient Maya civilization, who understood the path of the sun, were able to convince the masses that they could predict the equinoxes, the path of Venus, and the changing of the seasons.

So, too, our understanding and 'predicting' the future is actually based on the ability to understand established trends and understand how and when they will come to fruition in a world where chaos intervenes.

Because even in chaos there is a pattern – even if that pattern is that there is no pattern.

THE AVALANCHE AND THE BUTTERFLY EFFECT

A phrase I often use to describe the power of an idea is: "Every avalanche starts with the movement of a single snowflake."

As an idea is created and given depth and realism, others begin to recognize and build upon the vision even more, and the idea becomes an Attractor — a vision that is self-perpetuating.

For example, MIT meteorologist and founding father of deterministic chaos, Dr. Edward Lorenz, discovered that the smallest variables could result in drastic changes to weather systems, and the smallest disturbances could give rise to enormous weather systems in the midst of total tranquility.

It is this discovery that led him to eloquently describe how a seagull, flapping its wings, can alter the behavior of weather. In later lectures, the seagull image became a butterfly. And, in true "attractionary" form, other scientists began to build upon the metaphor of butterflies causing disturbances, leading to such weather events as tornadoes in Texas, and typhoons in Asia.

Today, we have the near-household term "Butterfly Effect," which is used to describe a scenario where a small variable can drastically affect the outcome of any given scenario.

Now, to be clear, they aren't necessarily saying that every butterfly creates a tornado. Great events are going to happen. But, there are small ways that we can alter, and even direct the path of the future — of *business* tornadoes, *market* hurricanes and other trends. Given the right circumstances and direction, we can even cultivate the growth and magnitude of such phenomena.

If you embrace my theory that the progression of the present to the future is a deterministic system, (building on Lorenz theory of deterministic chaos) then the same kind of principle applies to the future of business. And it's infinitely more measurable in the world of business. The story of corporate success is filled with such success stories where small events have great impact.

Take, for example, a company called Dropbox. According to Dropbox founder, Drew Houston, the idea was conceived after he repeatedly forgot his USB drive while he was a student at MIT. He says that existing services at the time "suffered problems with Internet latency, large files, bugs, or just made me think too much."

He began making something for himself, but then realized that it could benefit others with the same problem. Houston founded Dropbox, Inc. in 2007, and shortly thereafter secured seed funding from Y Combinator. Dropbox officially launched at 2008's TechCrunch50, an annual technology conference. The company now has over 4 million customers. A thriving business and a major innovation born from forgetting something as tiny as a USB drive.

Step 1: Build Your Vision

In short, when building your vision of the future, look for ways to recognize the butterflies in New York that start the typhoons in Asia. The goal is to catch those butterflies and set them free as attractors.

MATH AND THE ATTRACTOR

Attractor is term often used in math equations. In the world of mathematics, dynamic (or dynamical) systems are often graphically illustrated by a figure known as an attractor.

This attractor is a shape that forms when the results of dynamic equations are plotted over and over through a series of iterations. Over time, if we plot the answers to the equations after plugging in the variables, a shape begins to form. For a simple equation like 3+4, we know that there is a single answer, which is +7. It's a single point on an axis.

It follows then, that for a simple equation like this:

$$ax+by=c$$

The answer is represented as a straight line.

Now add a variable to the equation — something a little more complicated, like this:

$$y=ax^2+bx+c$$

You come up with a parabolic curve.

But if we try to come up with a mathematical representation of a dynamic and seemingly chaotic system using the number of variables involved (in say, the operations of a telecom company during its first two years of existence), the picture will appear more random, with dots appearing all over the grid.

Communicating with the Future

It may appear to be messy chaos, but there is still an order here. After repeated iteration, a pattern will emerge. This pattern is called an "Attractor."

Now, taking the term out of the strict mathematical sense, and applying it philosophically to the future — Attractors can be influenced, shaped, and to a certain extent, built.

By studying the present, and participating in the dynamic system of life, by playing an active part in the progression of present to future, true visionaries can actually affect the shape of things to come.

Our greatest areas of uncertainty include natural systems (like the weather, earthquakes, floods and animal/insect behavior) and human systems (like technology, government, economy, energy and human behavior).

Given that, our ability to manage and direct those systems is the key to controlling the future.

DaVinci was able to manage those systems by building *his* vision through art. He gave aeronautic designers something to build toward. He gave them a vocabulary of ideas. These visions of the future were the inspiration to thousands who attempted to build flying machines and to fulfill the dream DaVinci had inspired.

Translated into the language of the futurist, Leonardo created an Attractor.

An Attractor can be further explained as an event in the future that we are somehow drawn towards. We are being drawn towards the Attractors, like a force of nature. DaVinci, along with many others, helped turn the concept of flying into an attractor. As it was conceptualized, written about and illustrated, it became believable.

Step 1: Build Your Vision

Leonardo had staked his claim on the future.

IF YOU BUILD IT THEY WILL COME

Trends are often viewed as things that simply happen, things that come about as if from the ether. Others may see them as something to be chased. A futurist knows quite plainly that trends are made.

If want you to stake a claim on the future, explore it and exploit it as if it were a mining claim on the side of a nearby mountain. All that needs to be done is to go up that mountain and to start digging.

But before any shovels can hit the dirt, a trail must be forged. You need a way to get up that mountain. These types of pathways are abundant in many parks throughout the suburban areas of the United States. Often they lead to picnic areas, or waterfalls, or scenic overlooks.

People like to follow trails.

These winding trails and pathways often start out as those forged by animals on the search for food or shelter. After such a pathway has been blazed, it is common for humans to follow the path. This is generally because, well, it looks like a trail. With every footfall along this path, the trail becomes even more established. The pathway is, in a way, maintained and perpetuated by the foot traffic.

Before beginning your project, consider the path not yet blazed. Envision the journey before you take the first step. In fact, it would be best to assemble your creative professionals, and have them develop a vision of these paths before anyone sets forth up that mountain.

Then blaze those trails using ideas (short-story competitions and articles) and visuals (photos and film) — letting your creativity (and your creative team) dig a trend pathway toward the future.

That's where you stake a claim.

You stake a claim, like a mining claim of sorts. You put a stake in the ground somewhere in the future and that becomes an anchor point for decisions in your business. You create an Attractor.

There are eight kinds of attractors:

1. Inventions

2. Cures

3. Discoveries

4. Firsts

5. Challenges

6. Systems

7. Solutions

8. Standards

These are the end goals that we strive toward. They become the anchor points we work toward. Attractors are the trails that lead to the future.

So how do you create an Attractor? By asking the right questions.

Step 2: Create an Attractor

"What does the future want?"

Asking questions begins the cycle of Attractor formation, because purpose drives our quest for knowledge. To find meaning and purpose, we need more knowledge.

In today's world, information is infinite, but knowledge is finite.

According to a 2010 report by the Global Information Industry Center, the hours we spend consuming information has grown 2.6 percent per year from 1980 to 2008 to an average of nearly 12 hours per day.

At the same time, our ability to sort through the growing storehouses of information and find those shimmering glints of needles-in-the-haystack information is a relentless quest. It is a quest we cannot do alone. Our innovation takes over.

The more we know and understand about the vision and the trends surrounding it, the quicker and deeper our trail leads to the future.

50 INTERVIEWS

Recently, a friend of mine decided he was going to break away from corporate America and start his own business. As these things go, he sat down and discussed his plan with his wife. She told him that she thought his idea was great, but that there may be some gaps in his understanding of how this would truly be successful.

Just as wives are often typically more willing to ask for directions when lost, she applied the same thinking to his search for a new career path. She asked him to seek advice. But it didn't end there. She advised him to ask the opinions of 50 different professionals who had achieved a measure of success in the field he was pursuing.

Though it seemed a daunting task at first, as each interview was concluded, he began feeling a gain in momentum for the process. Each interview spawned many more questions for the next interview. Answers offered by some offered insight into how to approach the next subject.

Incidentally, I was number 46 on the list. When we were having our discussion, he was raring to go. He had a clear vision of what was ahead of him. What was apparent to me was that he had undergone a huge educational process. It was something that had garnered him more practical knowledge and professional contacts than if he had spent three times the number of hours sitting in a classroom.

Beyond that, this was one-on-one time with working professionals, in his desired field, who were flattered to be asked for their opinions. This simultaneously educated him and built a contact list of 50 people with whom he could begin building future professional relationships.

This process can work whether you're a 15-year-old who wants to be a magician, a youngster with aspirations to NASCAR, or a retiree looking to find a new career path. We benefit from the experiences of others. And there are many out there with rich experience and war stories that they are just bursting at the seams to share.

The point I am making here is that you build your own network of friends and colleagues as you go. This network can help you identify the "roads less traveled." Now, my friend is passing this knowledge, wisdom, and enthusiasm on as he helps coach others through the "fifty interviews" process.

The name of his business? Fifty Interviews.

POWER OF TEN

Creating an attractor requires looking at the roads traveled (trends) and identifying the opportunity for discovery (the treasure of the future). One trend I have noticed in the world of information gathering and processing illustrates what I like to call the power of ten.

We are able to gather and consume information at an exponentially greater rate than before. Imagine a set of questions based on widely available historical and topical knowledge of events. Nothing too hard, but these are questions just esoteric enough that they involve a bit of research.

Just twenty years ago, a set of questions might require the average person to get in his car, drive to the library, open the card catalog, access the microfiche collection, and hope that the answers would be there.

Going back further in time, before Gutenberg, before printing, and before transit, a young person seeking knowledge may require ten times the amount of time to access this same information.

With the advent of personal computers in every home hooked to the Internet, the amount of time required to access information jumped to about ten minutes.

Now, it would seem that the only thing holding us back from accessing information is the physical task of typing in a query in order to get our answers. At some point in the future, keyboards will go away, as we devise a faster interface between our brains and the cloud of information that's out there.

So, where you have a ten-minute response time now, you could easily whittle that down to ten seconds.

The idea here is not that we are necessarily becoming smarter, but that we are able to access outside information faster. And having access to this information doesn't mean we know what to do with it.

What is important is that we've identified a trend. Simply put, it's the idea that all of the "stuff" we need to use in order access information eventually goes away. So what does that make the future of information gathering look like? Much like the past flow of knowledge — through story.

Consider the keyboard in front of you every day. Here we can begin by building a base of storytelling.

I could ask you to make a technical diagram of what this non-keyboard interface looks like. You could gather a team to ask questions and offer ideas. The team you gather may then produce a

Step 2: Create an Attractor

series of videos with graphics on the design and usefulness of each interface.

You could also, as a project, ask the team to devise a small focus group on the effectiveness of the various models proposed in a design competition. The result is that the vision becomes real in the minds of the people who are designing the future and the people who are listening to the various pitches.

The new keyboard interface project just described is a perfect example of the identification of a trend and an opportunity to take ownership of it — to stake a claim on the future. In fact, we have devised and product-tested the efficacy of designs that don't exist for a challenge we are still years away from facing. This is the essence of planning and designing the future.

Furthermore, inside the minds of the designers and those listening, the mere process of building this vision of the future implants small particles of the future vision. We'll call these particles "Futurons." They are the multitude of little sticking points of thought that begin to form the Attractor. And through Attractors, we now know that we can create the future.

The Attractor then is the basic mechanism by which we can realize our designs of the future. It is a collection of ideas, visions, stories, and planned outcomes that gives a community something to strive toward. A touchstone, it can be a reminder of a common goal, and a visualization aid for those who contribute to its realization.

The airplane was the result of a fully realized attractor based on DaVinci's dream of flight in the past, while flying cars might be a good example of a current attractor.

SO WHERE IS MY FLYING CAR?

Most of us are still stuck on visions of George Jetson's bubble-shaped car buzzing across the television screen — remnants of Hanna-Barbera's hugely influential cartoon series, launched in 1962. Our first generation of mass-produced flying cars, however, will look far different from what George was driving.

Over the years, we have seen many versions of flying cars, starting with the Curtiss Autoplane in 1917. Decade after decade, designs have evolved along with the conceptual underpinnings of what constitutes a flying car.

In 2009 when Terrafugia launched the maiden voyage of its own flying car known as "The Transition," the universal reaction people voiced was, "Interesting, but it's not really a flying car." This was because the body still *looked* very much like an airplane.

NASA has begun referring to flying cars as PAVS (Personal Air Vehicles) and has attempted to differentiate them from other flying vehicles. NASA has also concluded that for any of these vehicles to become commercially successful, they need to meet the following criteria. They need to:

- Seat 2 to 6 passengers.
- Allow for a 150-200 mph (322 km/hr) cruising speed.
- Be quiet.
- Be safe.
- Be comfortable.
- Be reliable.
- Be able to be flown by anyone with a driver's license.
- Be as affordable as travel by a car or airliner.
- Include near all-weather vision capability enabled by Synthetic Vision Systems (NASA's term for a technology

with better-than-human visualization of the terrain and airspace).

- Be highly fuel efficient (able to use alternative fuels).
- Be able to fly long distances without needing to refuel.
- Provide "door-to-door" travel capabilities, via vehicle road ability, or small residential airfields or "vertiports" with only a short walk from the aircraft to the final destination.

Essentially, flying cars need to be as comfortable and convenient as cars that exist today. They also need to be extremely safe, and fly from Point A to Point B without human interference or folly.

Expanding on NASA's list, there are five key technological breakthroughs that will be needed for the first generation of flying cars to become viable:

1. FULLY AUTOMATED NAVIGATION SYSTEMS

    The average person has a difficult time navigating on a two-dimensional surface. The flying car industry will not be able to "get off the ground" without an onboard navigator that "handles the driving." Yes, people will want the freedom of being able to do some creative maneuvering in certain situations, but that will only be allowed in rare instances.

2. LOW-IMPACT VERTICAL TAKE-OFF

    When used by average person, flying cars can't have a runway requirement. They need to be able to take off and land vertically without blowing the leaves off of trees or shutters off of neighbor's windows.

3. CONVENIENT FLY-DRIVE CAPABILITY

As humanity makes the transition from ground-based autos to flying cars there will be a need for both driving on the ground and flying in the air.

4. SILENT ENGINES

Because there are no significant acoustical barriers in the air, the engines on flying cars will need to be virtually silent. Very few cities will want to put up with the noise of thousands of flying vehicles if they all sound like airplanes today.

5. SPECIALIZED SAFETY SYSTEMS

To date, both aircraft and airspace have been closely controlled by organizations like the FAA and the NTSB to ensure the safety of the flying public. Because of the sheer volume of vehicles being navigated by average drivers (read "untrained pilots"), additional safety measures will need to be in place. Required safety features will include such things as collision avoidance systems and drop-out-of-the-sky emergency airbags on the outside of the vehicles.

Additionally, with the potential for thousands of vehicles cluttering the airspace, one additional requirement will be that they become virtually invisible from the ground — a tall order indeed.

Step 2: Create an Attractor

THE NORMAN MATRIX – DIRECTIONAL LAYERING OF AIRSPACE

In addition to the technology built into the vehicles, we will also need to develop a workable air traffic control system for exponentially larger traffic volumes.

With several hundred thousand vehicles flying over a city, there will need to be an organized system for managing the traffic, and having all vehicles at a particular altitude traveling the same direction would eliminate many problems. This is an automated navigation system I've labeled the "Norman Matrix" (named after my dad.)

In the Norman Matrix, all vehicles traveling at 1,000-foot altitude will be traveling due north, at 1,010-foot altitude 1 degree east of due north, 1,020-foot altitude 2 degrees east of due north, etc. Vehicles will spiral up to make a right turn, or spiral down to make a left turn.

With a fully automated navigation system, this type of maneuvering should be invisible to the operator.

While not a perfect solution (the North Pole becomes a crash point for those flying due north), it does represent a good starting point for engineering a more comprehensive air traffic solution — an important advancement because there will be more than just cars hovering in the atmosphere.

COMING SOON – FLYING DELIVERY DRONES

As we look over the list of technologies needed, it becomes clear that virtually every aspect of the flying car era will also be needed for us to usher in a workable system for flying delivery drones. But it can be done without the dangers of flying people.

For us to reach a point where large numbers of average people can conveniently fly across town for work, school and shopping, we will need to spend a few years practicing with non-passenger drones. Once the drones have been perfected, we can easily transition to the flying car era.

Logically, companies such as FedEx or UPS should pioneer any full-scale drone delivery service. But as with most large companies, they tend to be more risk-averse than some of the private and small business innovators. Small companies will develop the prototypes, which the large companies will later use.

The U.S. military has been proving the viability of unmanned drones, with over 5,500 already being used in combat. However, most military drones, such as the Predator and Reaper, are designed to operate more like a plane requiring runways for takeoff and landing.

Delivery drones, like flying cars, need precise vertical takeoff and landing capabilities. For this reason, some of the innovative companies in the rapidly growing "quadricopter" field may be better positioned to move into this category. Quadricopters today are primarily used for surveillance and aerial monitoring.

Thinking beyond traditional deliveries, flying drones may be used to deliver water, change out the batteries on your home, remove trash and sewage, and even vacuum the leaves on your lawn. For some, the drones will allow them to live off the grid, and even off the net. But again, this is just a jumping off point — this vision is still being created.

CHANGING THE WORLD IN THE PROCESS

Once the volume of flying cars reaches a significant number, somewhere in the range of 500,000 to 1 million, countries will begin to lose control of their citizens.

When the Internet began to scale in the early 1990's, it did far more than transform communications. The viral nature of the World Wide Web began creating borderless economies, causing individual countries to lose control of commerce. The flying car will be just as powerful a revolution.

In addition to borderless commerce, the flying car creates confusion about issues related to power and control, even the sovereignty of nations.

Borders will become meaningless to people with flying cars. Yes, it will be possible for countries to develop electronic borders, but that will only create a black market for cloaking devices and invisibility shields.

Flying cars will do far more than transform transportation; they will transform government, taxation, conflict, commerce, culture, patriotism, and much more. As with any new technologies, not all of the changes will be good.

In the early days of the Internet, we could only begin to imagine the opportunities that would eventually accompany this kind of innovation. It will be the same with flying cars.

For me, the best way to phrase it is: "Flying cars will unleash our bodies in much the same way the Internet has unleashed our minds." And all from a vision built by cartoonists, pilots, engineers and dreamers like DaVinci.

Communicating with the Future

How do I know this you ask? And how am I able to "see the future? The answer is I have a pocket full of holes.

MY FIRST ENCOUNTER WITH HOLES

I spent my childhood on the edge of reality.

On the outside, I looked like a perfectly normal child, but on the inside my brain was filled with all sorts of ideas that were so crazy I felt I couldn't talk about them. Whenever I tried, people tended to laugh and ridicule me.

I was born and raised on a farm in South Dakota, so maybe it was my isolated childhood that caused all these ideas to happen. Maybe I was dropped on my head a few too many times as a baby. But whatever the reason, all I knew was that if someone else had the opportunity to step inside my head while I was sleeping, it would have been a total mind-warping adventure for them.

Most people go to sleep to get some rest, but I go to sleep to find my next adventure.

One night when I was 12 years old, I remember having a wrestling-match dream. This is one of those dreams that seemed so intensely real it caused me to spend the whole night wrestling with the bizarre concepts that were simultaneously insulting my intelligence, and revealing great truths about the world around me.

The dream I was having showed me how to make holes.

All night long I found myself making holes. One hole after another, after another. And they were all different.

Step 2: Create an Attractor

No, I wasn't making holes inside of anything or through anything. Instead, I was making some sort of magical holes for later use.

Throughout my dream I was filling my pockets with ready-to-use holes, and these holes gave me powers — the power of perception, the power of discernment, and most importantly, the power of understanding.

Whenever I came to a closed door, I could simply pull out a hole and insert it into the door, and I would see what was on the other side.

Whenever someone creepy was following me, I simply pulled out a hole, stretched it until it had reached the appropriate size, and threw it down on the ground so they would fall into it.

Everywhere I looked, I found more uses for my holes. I could look under things, I could see behind things, and if someone started arguing with me, I could even put holes in their arguments.

These holes that I was carrying in my pocket became my source of power. They became my muse, my source of creative inspiration — a rabbit hole to explore if you will — important because at the time exploration was not really encouraged by the conventional populace.

OUR SOCIETY OF INFORMATION GATEKEEPERS

Being raised as a child of the 1960s, it seemed that everything I wanted to know was somewhere else.

Information was hidden, locked up or protected by people whose job it was to prevent the rest of the world from seeing their information. The flow of ideas was being barricaded and imprisoned behind the walls of corporate and academic control, and only those who could afford it were granted the rights to see it.

The closest distance between me and the things I wanted to know was invariably through a series of gatekeepers on this toll-ridden information highway.

I needed my holes to see inside.

Our greatest enemy in life has always been the "unknown." Even today, with vast improvements in communications technology, we are constantly being blindsided by things we don't know.

We live in a cruel and unforgiving world. Yet we are continually being separated from the simple solutions that could prevent mass chaos and even death, by tollbooth operators whose job it is to extract payment from us for answers we don't yet even know exist.

And it costs us.

THE COST OF IGNORANCE

According to the USGS National Earthquake Information Center, the death toll for earthquakes in 2010 was 226,729, with 222,570 deaths occurring in Haiti, and additional deaths happening in Chili and Tibet.

Furthermore, 2008 was a disastrous year in Myanmar (Burma), where over 140,000 people were killed by a single storm – Cyclone Nargis.

The 2011 earthquake in Japan and the resulting tsunami has not only resulted in an enormous death toll, but also has spurred a series of problems with massive ripple effects extending around the world.

All of these disasters could have been greatly reduced if we had the ability to see the situation more clearly, and with a little forethought, to move people out of harm's way.

The cost of ignorance is staggering.

I find myself constantly wanting to ask Charles Darwin the question, "Why have we evolved so poorly?"

BECAUSE IGNORANCE IS BLISS

Yet for all the wringing of hands and lamenting of our own human limitations, there is also tremendous value in hiding behind the great unknown.

Yes, hidden in the clock-ticking minutes before life's greatest disasters are peaceful serene moments of people at their best — laughing, hugging and giving generously of themselves.

Even after a disaster, before anyone knows the extent of the damage, we see people instantly transformed from people-helping-themselves into people-helping-people mode. We suddenly think "less about us" and "more about them."

So while many have paid the ultimate price for ignorance, we can also view ignorance as a tremendous blessing. In a world seeking balance, we cannot live at peace without experiencing the extreme polar opposites.

If we had a lens that could give us a clear understanding of the inner workings of the Earth, how differently would we live our lives? What type of systems would we use to monitor it? And most importantly, who would control it?

THE COMPLEXITY OF THE HOLE

As I mentioned earlier, my toolkit as a futurist consists of a pocket filled with magical holes.

Every time I peer through one of my holes, I gain a new perspective. In much the same way photographers change lenses on their cameras to gain a new perspective, my holes allow me to see the world with insights and revelations not afforded to others.

In this moment of full disclosure, revealing the secrets I once said would never be revealed, here are a few of the remarkable holes that I typically have poised and ready for use:

- SEE-THROUGH HOLE

  Perhaps the most useful of my holes is the one that enables me to see through walls, doors, and even inside metal file cabinets. Okay, maybe not really. The point is that I don't stop looking for answers. The impossible is always possible.

- MOVABLE HOLE

  Distance is relative when you have insight, but very often the answer you are seeking lies only a few inches away from the place you're looking. That is why the movable hole is so valuable. Simply move the hole and you will find your answer.

Step 2: Create an Attractor

- DATA-ENCRYPTION HOLE

  Sometimes I have to adjust the viewing angle of the hole, and even twist it a few times to bring it into focus, but even the best encryption is no match for a truly gifted hole-user.

- ANSWER HOLE

  Behind every situation that causes us to ask "why," is an answer. Staring through an Answer Hole is a very revealing experience when *we know the right questions to ask.*

- BACKWARD-LOOKING HOLE

  Too often what we think is *in front* of us is actually *behind* us. The real trick is to know whether to look forward or backwards.

- STRETCHER HOLE

  If your perspective is too small, the best option may be a stretcher hole to expand your thinking. However, in most cases, the perspective is far too big, requiring a much smaller hole to bring things into focus.

- NANO HOLES

  The problem with nanotechnology is remembering where you put your work. Remember, that the devil is always in the details, and details are far smaller than most people can imagine.

- SLOW HOLE

  Very often the answers I am seeking are traveling far too fast, so a "slow hole" will slow things down to just the right speed. Stop and smell the flowers. Sometimes all it takes to discover new things is time and quiet deliberation.

- HIDDEN-AGENDA HOLE

When trying to understand politics, few holes are more useful than the "hidden agenda hole." Motivations and agendas are often layered into the complex intermeshed turmoil happening inside many of our key decision-makers. This one takes practice because there is seldom just one agenda in play.

- FUTURE-VISION HOLE

Today, as I spend time studying our relationship with the future, I love nothing more than being able to reach into my pocket, pull out a "future-vision hole," and place it between me and this field of knowledge that separates us from the future. Based on what we know now, we can create and control the future.

Now I know what you're thinking. "Why do you get to use magical holes and not me?" and "If you really have magical holes, why are you wrong so much of the time?"

To answer your first question, these holes can be dangerous. As Stan Lee, creator of Spiderman, once said, "With great power comes great responsibility." I am taking a great risk even revealing these holes exist. So no, you can't have them. And don't ask me if you can borrow one because the danger is far too great.

As for the second question, I have never been granted the ability to see the big picture, just pieces of it. And my ability to extrapolate the missing pieces is often fraught with misdirects and misguided conjecture leading to wrong-headed conclusions.

What I am still missing is the ability to create a hole-within-a-hole, a simultaneous big-picture, little-picture hole. There is exponentially greater power that can be unleashed with overlapping holes; ones that will enable me to have a backward-looking, future-vision hole that is concurrently stationary and movable, permanently square but with flexible, stretchable sides, combining the powers of fast and slow into a left-handed, right-handed multi-perspective hole that I can call upon on at a moment's notice.

No, I don't have that one yet, but I can always dream. I'm building my vision for that right now. I haven't lost my childhood "wonder" and neither should you.

THE MUSEUM OF FUTURE INVENTIONS

Consider George Lucas. As an engineer on a project known as "Star Wars" in the 1980s, I can bear first-person witness to the filmmaker's impact upon our late Cold War race in the sky. The same can also be said for such visionaries as Gene Roddenberry, Phillip K. Dick, and Neal Stephenson. These great storytellers have shaped our world. So, rather than simply revering them, why not emulate them?

If storytelling has brought us this far into the future, why not develop this method to work on a more focused and specific scale? If we approach the development of a company in the same way a movie plot is developed, we stretch our minds in new directions, while fostering an engaging corporate culture that is exciting to participate in.

Yes, I am advocating the use of storytelling, storyboarding, and video production, and all manner of creative production in the development of business. The following chapters will outline methods, tools, and techniques for creating this visionary culture within organizations of all shapes and sizes. A solo entrepreneur will find useful information, and so will a startup team or a COO of a corporation with hundreds of employees. But it is more than simply getting a bunch of people together and having them shout ideas. It's a method requiring focus, organization, incentive and immersion.

I had this brainstorm one night about future inventions. I thought, "Wouldn't it be cool to write a book about all the big things that still need to be invented?" I kept rolling that around in my head.

I thought, "Wouldn't that be cool if you had created this compendium of all the big things that still need to be accomplished? And then a college student that's graduating from college could come to this resource and someone who is looking for their calling in life they could go paging through it. And suddenly one of these items would click with them and they would say 'ah, that's the one; that's the one I want to orient my life around.' "

As I kept ruminating on that idea, as I kept brainstorming it, I realized that books, for ideas like this, end up being at some level too one-dimensional. You need to add more detail to it.

So I considered that what would be far better than just writing a book about it would be to actually create this museum of future inventions. I then spent a lot of time think about how would we go about creating this museum of future inventions.

So I came to this idea of developing a process for creating exhibits for this museum. It's very similar to what I've been describing: you have a future invention, you create a technical description of it, you send it off to three or four different storytellers. Then once the stories come back, you send those stories off to graphic artists. And the graphic artists then create these visuals. And so you have the stories, you have the graphic artwork and that creates three or four walls of an exhibit.

Step 2: Create an Attractor

And then you could start adding other elements. You could start creating a physical model, you could add animations, and you could start doing video pieces. You could even get to the point that you would start interviewing famous people about this technology.

So you interview Ted Turner or you interview Donald Trump or Steve Jobs or any number of other famous people. Then you would create the narrative that goes with all this. Based on all those interviews and all the information, you have this whole concept kind of comes to life. And you have a museum exhibit based on that whole body of work that's being created.

You have, as a result, begun to influence the future.

So what is the next step in your ability to see the future? How do you get from asking questions and gathering information based on trends?

How do you get from rough sketches (like those dreamt up by DaVinci and Hanna Barbera) to the reality of lift off? By publishing your vision.

Step 3: Unleash Your Vision

"The future is created in the minds
of the people around us."

Leonardo DaVinci spent his final years as a frustrated man. He maintained a relentless passion to change the world, yet his primary tools for making these changes were nothing more than sketchpads and canvas.

All told, DaVinci dedicated over 500 drawings and 35,000 words to the concept of flying — a persisting dream of his that wouldn't be realized for some 300 years in a hot air balloon field and then following 400 years of flyable aircraft.

So why did it take so long?

Leonardo was indeed a popular person during his time, but popularity only reached so far. Gutenberg was still tinkering with his printing press, and there was no other form of mass communication.

Step 3: Unleash Your Vision

The DaVinci name was not all that well known across Europe. Consequently, his ideas were not common knowledge, and the DaVinci-inspired flying machines would have to wait centuries before they could be combined with enough other ideas to construct a workable prototype.

Ideas don't self-perpetuate.

Most of the world's greatest accomplishments are the result of thousands of smaller ideas coming together in one place and one time. Typically there is one person, one inventor, one lone driving force working like a chef in a kitchen to mix the idea-ingredients in the right proportions, and stir them up in a bowl, to make something deliciously brilliant happen.

So once you have conceptualized your idea, you must add dimension and detail to add realism.

Much like advertising agencies trying to influence our wants, needs, and desires for present-day products, we must build momentum on a subconscious level for visions that currently exist only in the minds of visionaries.

Let's take another look back.

We didn't need mouthwash and deodorant until we found out that we do indeed *stink*. Influencing us through our desire to be attractive and confident, advertising agencies have convinced us that our own natural odor is offensive to those around us (and even ourselves). The need to not smell like, well, ourselves has become very real.

And now that we are bombarded with messages about smelling good, looking good and feeling good every day — the battle has begun.

THE BATTLE FOR YOUR MIND

Influence is power. Clergymen, columnists and teachers have it. Even butchers at grocery stores have it. What they do is hold your attention better than most and engender trust. They are "super influencers," and they are all around you.

We are social creatures who shape our lives, lifestyles, consumer habits and beliefs according to the influences and influencers in our lives. We can usually name the most influential people we know. We quickly can point to songs and films that made us think, laugh, cry or change. By the same token, we all have a private fan club, groups of people who care about and listen to us.

You have "fans," or a group that expands and contracts as your personal charisma and the power of what you have to say waxes and wanes. In the advertising media world, influence is measured by how many people listen and/or act.

The job offers you receive, the business opportunities that come your way, and the people you meet are all influenced by the relationships you have built. Your ability to manage and influence your fan club will determine, to a large extent, where you end up on your life's journey.

This idea is nothing new. Fan clubs are as old as culture itself, dating back to days long before fanatical teenagers fell in love with hip-swinging rock stars. And, worship didn't always involve people. Some fan clubs develop around ideas, themes, trades or even industries — space elevator enthusiasts come to mind.

Influence is as old as tribes. Influence powerfully transcends what other considerations may preoccupy us at a given time. An "influencer" is a person who not only wants you to care about them or an institution, but they want to sway your thinking, to call you to action, and recruit others to a cause.

Influence is commodity-like, too. It can be borrowed as an author might do when citing an expert to show authority. You can enlist fans by making reference to experiences surrounding an image, personality, brand, and charisma of the influencer. Elite athletes like Olympic medalists and NFL quarterbacks are paid a king's ransom for endorsements showing that complete strangers can gain our trust, and influence us.

YOU HAVE THE POWER TO INFLUENCE THE FUTURE

Who are your primary influencers? Who is it that you pay most attention to when they recommend something?

Major media still invests heavily in salaries for news people who have built reputations over time and earned trust in smaller markets. Bylined staff writers and others who populate traditional media were the few, the elite. You could count the number of major news outlets on one hand. There were television stations, radio stations and the various publications that populated newsstands.

Today, the number of offerings has exploded with online media, podcasts, satellite radio, downloadable books, and somewhat devious influencers such as TV shows with sneaky attempts at product placement.

In the 2000 edition of *Positioning* by Al Ries and Jack Trout, the authors cite the statistic that America consumes 57 percent of all of the advertising in the world. This shouldn't surprise us. The wealthiest nation is also home to the largest concentration of media in the world.

There is no escaping advertisement. We are under a constant barrage of competing marketing messages. Even ads positioned on bathroom walls offer no refuge from the onslaught of pitches.

Media of the last century used a shotgun approach to marketing, spraying a large demographic area with pellet messages intended for all, but they would strike only a tiny percentage.

This expensive and wasteful type of marketing will begin to vanish. Trying to shape a message that resonates with as many people as possible is an underappreciated art — that is until you win a cool million for your Doritos commercial (like the ones that aired during the 2009 Super Bowl). Madison Avenue is still smarting from that assault on their pride, as simple videos created by the general public were highly successful. They should get used to getting bested by the little guys.

Over time, the geek-laden "Numerati" – so aptly labeled in Steve Baker's recent book, (aptly titled *The Numerati*) – will devise systems for targeting ideal customers. Armed with the exacting precision of next-generation digital targets they will increase the percentage who respond to a message from the 1 percent range of today's direct marketing pieces to conceivably as high as 50 percent. The response rate will rise. Perhaps most reassuringly, the other 50 percent won't feel that a constant barrage of misdirected ads is nagging them.

ADVERTISING AS A POPULARITY CONTEST

Just as people maintain concentric circles of relationships, they also manage and direct concentric circles of influence. Each circle of association starts with the strongest rapport close to us and extends out to weaker and weaker relationships.

Today's technology tools allow marketers to extend their reach far beyond anything we could have dreamed of 20 years ago, and the barrier to entry today is nearly non-existent.

The gatekeepers can join buggy whip makers in history's unemployment line. "Getting the word out" will be done by anyone interested in sharing information. Things as simple as a blog entry, Facebook or Twitter post, Flickr photo, or YouTube video are grabbing audience attention as never before, in numbers that have marketers running to social media boot camps.

Social media experimentation is producing some interesting projects, turning social networking into a popularity contest. Many become confused by the sheer power of social media, finding themselves suddenly out of their element when it comes to leveraging popularity and influence. Even as they reach the lofty levels of 20,000 or even 50,000 followers on Twitter, the proud owners of these accounts find that they are unable to cash in. Their massive numbers don't translate to influence.

Product recommendations and personal endorsements made by someone with no credentials other than a large follower-base tend to fall on deaf ears. Perhaps there are few genuine followers among so many leaders. Meanwhile, someone with 1,000-2,000 followers can have a disproportionate influence in social media, building an audience of readers who hang on their every word.

We are in the early stages of social media experimentation. No one is taking bets on the value of a Twitter account with 50,000 followers – yet. And certainly not on the value of that account five years from now.

In the future, so-called super-influencers will begin to undergo massive scrutiny to accurately parse the profile and makeup of each swayable impression, assigning value to each potential conversion. In short, influencers will soon need to know their own metrics.

FUTURE TRENDS DEFINING THE FUTURE OF INFLUENCE

As we think through the trend lines that will govern tomorrow's influence brokers, we begin to see a radically different world emerging. As you are determining ways to publish your vision, consider:

- THE DECLINING ROLE OF TELEVISION

    As the battle for attention escalates, the television industry will find itself ill-prepared to compete with the emerging Internet-based video businesses. Television executives will watch their markets decline rapidly as competition for ad dollars surfaces from industries as diverse as gaming and online cooking channels, to virtual worlds, social networking, and even hybrid programs we've never imagined.

Step 3: Unleash Your Vision

- ## THE DECLINING ROLE OF THE PRINTED WORD

  The market for ink-on-paper forms of written material will shrink rapidly in the coming years. The life of newspapers, magazines and books in their current form as a physical paper product will quickly diminish and be replaced with their digital counterparts viewable through handheld devices such as book readers, tablets, iPhones, Android phones, and more. The written word will live on for many years, but more as a digital medium than as a physical one.

- ## AN INCREASE IN INTERACTIVE INFLUENCE

  There has been a growing disdain for one-way, top-down forms of communication. Printed material is a perfect example. If a reader objects to a printed statement or comment, there is little recourse for voicing an objection. However, in the digital world, nearly every channel has been set up as interactive two-way communication, and the feedback loop is in real time. Influence becomes more authentic and credible when it is voiced in an open forum.

- ## THE PARTICALIZATION OF MARKETS

  As WIRED Magazine's editor Chris Anderson has predicted, the mass consumer markets have splintered into millions of tiny long tail markets, each delineated by its unique micro-customer base and specific sphere of influence.

- ## THE CREATION OF NEW MEDIA CHANNELS

Within the past 10 to 15 years, several new media channels have come into existence including YouTube, Facebook, Twitter, Second Life, Digg, LinkedIn, Flickr, iTunes, Amazon, Bebo, Friendster, MySpace, Reddit, Revver, Wordpress, Veoh, Daily Motion, Blogger, Spike and many more. Most of these channels have created features that allow a person to expand their own sphere of influence within that channel.

- ## THE 8,000 POUND GORILLA

With all the new media channels coming into play, the 8,000-pound gorilla that has emerged is Google. Leveraging its dominant position in the global search market and combining it with an assortment of sophisticated tools such as AdWords, AdSense and Analytics, Google has become a prevailing presence online, leaving other contenders such as Yahoo and Microsoft with respectable but far less influential roles. Even though Google is on top, its position is that of the conduit for influence, and the company has proved that there is a tremendous amount of money to be made in giving people the keys to their own empire of influence.

- ## THE GROWING MARKETS FOR NICHE INFLUENCERS

Companies are figuring out ways to define their target markets with ever-greater precision. In doing so, they will be wanting to align themselves with the "big fish in the small pond," knowing that the efficiency of gaining new customers will exceed anything they have ever tried in the past. Companies wishing to tap into a market defined as male, lovers of Italian food, fishing, boating, football, who

50

play backgammon, and watch the TV show "Lost," can probably find blogs and YouTube channels that are a perfect match.

- THE EMPIRE OF ONE INFLUENCERS

  The vast majority of media moguls in the future will run their business as one-person operations. Most of their operation will be run as a loose affiliate of networks with content being produced all over the world, distributed to the audience controlled by the individual empire business owner.

- THE OPPORTUNITY TO CROSS MEDIUM BARRIERS

  Thought leaders in the webinar industry are rarely the same as thought leaders on YouTube, Flickr, blogs, Twitter, podcasts, Kinect, or Facebook. As each of these platforms continues to develop, the level of detail to the obsessive-minded turbo-influencer will become all-consuming.

- DEATH OF THE GENERALIST

  While there will be many exceptions to the rule, people who are experts in a specific niche will fare far better than people who are talented generalists. Each media channel is trending toward increasingly sophisticated tools. In the future, colleges will begin to offer degrees in YouTube programming, Google AdWords marketing, blog journalism and much more.

Even though we have seen many new options come into play, some of the old structures for peddling influence are still alive and well. As an example, an expert speaking on stage to a captive audience is still incredibly powerful. Being a persuasive writer, radio talk show host, or industry expert still has great value and will continue to be valuable in the foreseeable future.

SO WHAT COMES NEXT?

In the past, the owner of a small-town newspaper had a very well-defined community where the town limits defined the market of the time. Today we are seeing physical boundaries disappear. However, new boundaries are forming around the various media we are employing.

Additionally, crossing political boundaries, language barriers and time zone differentials are all past problem areas that are dissolving around us. Rising instead are communities of interest where people are forming bonds around technologies, sports, competitions, and literally millions of other micro-points of fascination.

Here are a few other thoughts on the trends we will see:

- LIMITED ATTENTION SPANS

  The most-watched videos on YouTube are 30 seconds and shorter. Even though it doesn't seem like our attention spans can get any shorter, they will. People who can put together "charticles" (charts that tell an entire story), short animations, graphics and videos that can convey a message in the shortest amount of time will be in high demand in the coming years.

- INCREASED FREQUENCY

  It's best not to think about influence from a "lights-on" vs. "lights off" perspective. Rather, influence tends to act more like pulsing power with every surge tied to your latest contribution followed by a period of waning interest. A person's or company's position as an influencer will be determined not only by the potency of its effort but increasingly by its frequency of contribution.

- EXPANDED COURSEWARE TOOLS

The business world has long accepted that any person can create a course and market it to businesses. Our ability to create courses for the rest of the education market is coming. Several companies are working to create "rapid courseware building tools," and we will see several new markets for extending influence springing to life as a result of this in the coming years. For examples, explore sites like learnable.com, Udemy.com and Sophia.com.

- EXPANDED APPLICATIONS

When it comes to mobile apps, we are experiencing a sea of change in attitudes as to how we view the world.

It's just a matter of months before the number of available apps will exceed the number of available books in print.

Apps are a piece of information that we interact with on a far different basis than a traditional book. They serve many purposes and enter our lives from thousands of different angles.

- LESS TEXT-BASED SOCIETY

In coming years, the written word will begin to lose appeal as other forms of media such as video, podcasts, animations and others become easier to work with. The first major turning point will come when keyboards start to disappear. This will be a clear sign of the diminishing power of the written word.

- MORE PERVASIVE INTERNET

Traveling across the U.S. and trying to stay connected to the Internet is painful at best. Current efforts under way should fix connectivity issues in even the most remote locations, and connection speeds should amp up to truly mesmerizing levels over the coming decade.

- DEVELOPED HOLOGRAPHY

At one time, it was believed we would instantly spring from our present two-dimensional world into a lifelike 3D media where it was impossible to tell the real life from its projection counterpart. But holography has been far more difficult to implement than its proponents imagined, and we now know that it will be introduced in baby-stepped nuances, with each version becoming a bit more lifelike than the past.

That said, the 3D world is still coming, and we will begin to see improved elements of "three dimensionality" showing up in everything from games to graphics and videos. The allure of realism will attract followers slowly at first but gain speed quickly over the next decade.

The industry that will form around the concept of influence is a fluid ocean of moving parts, with each current of opportunity morphing and overlapping onto other currents on a daily basis. This is a sport where only the most agile can play, and maintaining your position as a super influencer will be a constant struggle. The smaller the niche, the greater your chances are of survival — *of making your vision real.*

DON'T JUST KEEP IT REAL, MAKE IT REAL!

Realism creates viability. It pays then, to create a purpose for your vision and develop a body of work around that specific topic. This body of work may include:

- Short stories

- Graphic art

- Animations

- Models

- Surveys

- Interviews

- Videos

As the vision is being created, a treasure trove of intellectual property can be staked out including:

- Patents

- Trademarks

- Copyrights

TAKING OWNERSHIP OF THE FUTURE

In 2008, I spent the better part of a day with John Doll, who then was the Commissioner for Patents at the U.S. Patent and Trademark Office (USPTO). Four years earlier, an article I had written suggesting the USPTO open a branch office in Denver caught the attention of the Governor's office, and I was asked to head up a task force to look into it.

After a series of events the idea began to get some traction.

Commissioner Doll was in Denver, at our request, to hear Colorado's bid for a branch office, and I had the honor of accompanying him to several of the day's events. We carefully filled his day with a number of strategic high-level meetings, culminating in a reception on a perfect-weather day at the Governor's Mansion.

As our limo was making its way between meetings, I posed a question to the Commissioner, "Does the patent office view themselves as being in the business of selling patents?"

The reaction I got was a rather quizzical look. So I went on to explain.

"The U.S. Mint has taken on the attitude that they are in the business of selling coins, and they've been doing one hell of a job by creating new quarters for every state and a variety of new dollar coins.

Coin sales have gone through the roof. But my sense is that since the USPTO has such a massive backlog of patents in the queue (upwards of 1 million patents pending at that time), that no one is really looking at the upward marketing potential for new patents."

Step 3: Unleash Your Vision

Doll's first reaction was to go with the quality-first argument. "Our mandate is to make sure we perform a thorough examination of every application, so that is our primary objective."
Pressing the issue further, I continued. "If, for example, the latency period for patents dropped from 3 years to 3 weeks, you would sell a lot more patents.

Businesses would apply for far more patents, and since each patent that is awarded by the USPTO yields roughly $10,000 in fees over the life of the patent, the resulting revenue stream would be massive."

As a "free-enterpriser," this logic made perfect sense to me.

He went on to explain that since the USPTO had between 700,000 and 1 million patents waiting to be processed, it was difficult to envision taking on more work. Additionally, since the USPTO wasn't in charge of its own budget, it would be difficult to manage the resources necessary to handle more patent applications.

More money coming in would not work its way into the operating budget without congressional approval. So without additional staff, the agency would likely end up in crisis mode.

Clearly, Congress hadn't thought this one through. It was also clear that the budget topic was a real sore spot within the agency.

At the time some fast-track systems were being experimented with, and they were working to reduce the number of claims any one patent could make. But suggesting a three-week patent process was borderline insanity.

UNDERSTANDING THE PATENT GAME

For inventors who wish to license their patent as soon as possible, speed is of the essence. But for others, knowing their technology is far ahead of the curve and that it will take a long time for the rest of the world to catch up, speed works against them.

Every patent requires a different strategy, and the system's current time delays only complicate matters.

Truth be told, most patents that generate money do so in the last few years of their 20-year life span. That said, only a small percentage of patents generate any money at all.

When it comes to staking a claim on the future through the use of various intellectual property tools, the strategy can be a double-edged sword.

Going through this process, it is easy to find areas to patent, copyright or trademark. For some technologies, that may be the perfect approach. But for others, it can stop momentum in its tracks.

The speed with which technology gets developed can be greatly affected by the layers of ownership that get placed around the original idea. Even though it's possible to make a sizable income from a single patent, for breakthrough technologies an early patent application will likely involve premature thinking, erroneous claims, and simply bad judgment.

In the world of licensing, getting a license for patents is not like licensing a song, a photo or a video clip. There is no reason it couldn't be, but rarely are deals structured that way. A typical patent license requires attorneys staring across the table from each other with the billing meter ratcheting upward in the background.

For people choosing to go down the intellectual property path, it is best to work with a good attorney and weigh the options carefully.

OTHER WAYS OF STAKING A CLAIM

Another strategy works on the theory that almost more important than the legal ties to idea ownership are the emotional ways people connect to it.

Any individual, organization or business where the ideas and work projects become inextricably interwoven with the people driving them will create something akin to a "we're on a mission" form of leadership, and a certain segment of society has a natural tendency to follow anyone wanting to lead them on a well-inspired adventure.

Future visions will require leaders to drive them forward. Early-stage ideas, similar in some respects to a young child, will require unusually high levels of coddling and attentiveness. But over time, given the right amount of leadership, packaging, storyline and community, the vision will become self-perpetuating.

In this context, taking ownership of the future requires being the curator of the vision. In much the same way that plants need water, air and nutrients to thrive, a vision requires a special form of nurturing to make it self-perpetuating. The good news is that once there is a sufficient body of work, the vision does become self-perpetuating, increasing your influence and the likelihood that you are controlling the future.

It becomes what I refer to as the "Familiarity Contraction Principle," meaning that the more we know about the future, the easier it becomes for us to interact with it.

THE FAMILIARITY CONTRACTION PRINCIPLE

The first time a person gets into a car and drives to someplace new, the discovery process causes a heightened sense of awareness and the perception that time has slowed down.

Each subsequent trip to that same destination involves fewer discoveries, less awareness, and the perception of less time spent to get there.

After enough trips, our brain goes on autopilot, and our sense of time collapses even further.

Taken together, this entire phenomenon comprises the Familiarity Contraction Principle, and it paints a pretty good picture of the futurist outlook.

The "Familiarity Contraction Principle" is a concept that explains the perceived reduction in time, but it also explains how our familiarity with a specific outcome or goal will increase both the likelihood that it will happen and the efficiency with which it will occur.

As we increase the body of information surrounding a specific aspect of the future, we increase our familiarity with it. Our ability to plan and manage our own future is directly related to how familiar we are with it, and that is where we can begin to uncover some truly profound insights.

First, a little background. The idea of the Familiarity Contraction Principle was initially proposed by Drew Crouch, a good friend and inspiring top-level executive at Ball Aerospace, during one of our monthly meetings at the DaVinci Institute where we set out to solve some of the great problems of the world.

Step 3: Unleash Your Vision

Drew made the observation that driving from Boulder to Denver always takes longer than it seems, simply because we've made this trip so many times. Our perception of time seems to collapse along with our familiarity.

Our initial discussion was surrounding the perceived reduction in driving time, but upon even further reflection, the implications began to grow.

Side Note: The only known exception to this rule is driving through Kansas. For some reason, Kansas is a state that doesn't let your brain go onto autopilot, and each trip is as long as the first. Maybe even longer. But I digress... (I just like to pick on Kansas).

FOUNDATIONAL BRICKS OF FAMILIARITY

As you will soon see, familiarity is an enormously valuable tool that can be applied to countless situations, including a more realistic perspective for a vision of the future — making even the impossible or absurd less absurd and more possible.

Here are two examples that better explain how familiarity works:

1. When entering a dark room, our first instinct is to search for directional cues. If there is a small amount of light, our impulse is to look for visual cues. Once we've decided how much we can rely on visual information, we move on to our other senses, looking for auditory signals, smells, things we can touch and perhaps even taste.

   If it is a room we have been in before, we quickly race through our memory cells to correlate known information with whatever new information we are uncovering.

61

Once we reach the other side of the room, we have methodically logged everything we found to be pertinent, so any subsequent trip can take place in far less time.

The speed with which we can move through a dark room is directly related to how familiar we are with it.

2. A person who works on an assembly line is well aware of the efficiencies that can be gained through repetition.

    The craftsmen who work on building clocks gain tremendous efficiency between the first time a clock is built and the hundredth time. After multiple iterations of the same routine, an assemblyperson instinctively knows where to reach for each subsequent part. They learn how best to grasp and position the new parts to ensure the gears are aligned and components are properly seated.

    Over time the movements become fluid and instinctive. There is little brainpower needed for each new assembly as the brain shifts into autopilot and the person doing the work simply "zones out," letting their mind wander as their body goes through the motions. Every manufacturing plant manager is well aware of the value of familiarity.

3. When children are first introduced to the alphabet, they are shown the letters repeatedly to improve "familiarity" between the character shape and the corresponding sounds used to form words.

    The slow methodical process of connecting brain cell to brain cell is an exercise in familiarity building and also an essential part of learning.

    Over time, the micro-decisions needed to distinguish characters becomes second nature and our brains jump quickly past the individual letters and see the character groupings only as complete words.

MORE FAMILIARITY PRINCIPLES

Here are a couple other ways forces associated with familiarity have been demonstrated:

Exposure Effect - People tend to develop a preference for things merely because they are familiar with them. In studies of interpersonal attraction, the more often someone sees a person, the more pleasing and likable that person appears to be. Similarly, mere exposure typically reaches its maximum effect within 10-20 presentations, and some studies even show that liking may decline after a longer series of exposures. For example, people generally like a song more after they have heard it a few times, but multiple repetitions can reduce this preference.

Hindsight Bias - The hindsight bias states that people perceive certain events to be more predictable after the fact than they seemed before they had occurred. Often people believe that a disaster could have been avoided when they are actually misattributing familiar knowledge to a time before it was available.

FAMILIARITY – IT'S NOT JUST ABOUT THE PAST

Contrary to popular thinking, familiarity is not just about the past. Rather, our ability to develop a greater level of awareness and familiarity about the future can give us a significant competitive advantage.

Communicating with the Future

Every vision of the future begins as a vague concept. If there is enough meat on the bones, the idea will begin to grow. But the traditional path for letting ideas grow by themselves tends to be extraordinarily slow. Weeks turn into months and months often turn into decades as ideas languish in their own inability to reach the minds that most need them.

In much the same way a bad food system fails to provide the needed food and nourishment to starving people in remote areas, our idea network has suffered from broken patterns and constant disconnects.

An idea left to survive on its own has little chance of enduring. But an idea combined with hundreds or even thousands of similar or related ideas can quickly reach the point of critical mass.

THE FUTURE AS A FRAMEWORK

Done correctly, idea clusters create their own center of gravity. If we create a vision of the future and couple it with the right mechanisms for attracting other ideas, suddenly it takes on a life of its own.

To better illustrate this concept, think of any future concept as a piece of papier-mâché that starts with a wire framework. Each new idea serves as another piece of paper added to the frame, giving it mass, dimension and realism. Over time, the original collection of wires becomes a visual, touchable finished work that we can both physically and intellectually interact with.

Similarly, if we start with some future concept and start telling stories about it, adding illustrations, animations, videos, surveys and interviews, the entire body of work surrounding the original idea creates its own gravitational pull, making it an attractor.

Step 3: Unleash Your Vision

So how do you know if you've published your vision successfully? That requires some analysis – which leads us to Anticipatory Analytics.

Step 4: Review Your Results

"Thinking about the future will cause it to change."

Create exactly what the future wants, and the future will happen even faster. How can you do this? By using Anticipatory Analytics — a tool that I have devised for "communicating with the future."

Communication, in its most basic form, is nothing more than a signal sent out and a signal received. By unleashing the vision as described in the previous step, we are sending out a signal in the present for people to receive in the future. These visions will be tagged with unique keyword phrases for us to monitor.

We can view these as the "signal sent."

Once people have immersed themselves with the concepts and visions, and start integrating the keyword phrases into their daily conversations, we can begin to assess the impact they are having. By monitoring keyword usage through Google searches and with other tools, we can evaluate both short- and long-term effects.

Step 4: Review Your Results

This is the "signal received."

All visions of the future can be tagged with unique keyword phrases. Once the number of these phrases reaches critical mass inside of the "global conversation," we can use these keyword phrases in analysis to determine two things:

1. When the vision will become self-perpetuating.

2. When the market is ready for products related to that vision.

These anticipatory analytics can help shape the vision, so that we are providing what the future wants. By doing so, we increase the momentum of our vision.

A FAST MOVING FUTURE

Technology is the engine propelling time compression. While the overall trend began over 150 years ago with the introduction of time zones, it got a big boost in the 1940s with the introduction of fast food and the microwave oven, instant photography, and commercial airliners.

Computer technology raised the bar further when Moore's Law and its 24-month cycles moved the product development needle from steady to fast. Kids growing up in the new gadget world evolved into adept multi-taskers, with computer-driven solutions making things happen faster.

In the 1920s, the average U.S. adult slept 8.8 hours each day. By 2001 that figure had declined to 6.8, fully two hours less, according to the NIH. Thirty-four percent of lunches are eaten on the run, according to National Eating Trends, a trend fueled by the $112 billion U.S. fast-food business. Speed dating is now having a major impact on the dating scene. Sixty-six percent of people today watch TV while simultaneously surfing the web. Understanding time compression is one of the keys to unlocking future consumer behavior.

A survey by Reuters demonstrates the anxiety people have by living in today's fast-paced society:

- 49% felt they were unable to keep up with the flow of information.
- 43% were having trouble making important decisions because of data overload.
- 38% said they waste substantial amount of valuable time trying to locate needed information, and
- 33% suffered from stress-related health problems brought on by too much information.

But that isn't to say that repetition of key information is not valuable — especially when the goal is to control the future. Trailblazing is necessary, but it takes even more than that to make sufficient impact — recognizing what the future wants and answering that desire.

THE DAY OF THE DRONE IS UPON US

I make the argument that if we create a sufficient body of work around a particular topic, then we create an Attractor and society becomes drawn to that endpoint.

That argument runs into problems when you ask, "Where is my flying car? Where is my jetpack?"

Step 4: Review Your Results

If you do a Google search on the topic of "flying cars," you uncover roughly 20 million websites that talk about flying cars.

A similar search on "jetpacks" will yield over 1.3 million results.

With these two topics there is already a huge body of work in place, so why don't we already have commercially available flying cars and workable jetpacks?

There are two primary reasons. One is that these are both extremely complicated engineering problems with tens of thousands of failure points along the way. And two, no one has really taken ownership of the process.

Flying cars will require automated navigation systems, new kinds of vertical takeoff and landing technology, and an entire new traffic management system that the FAA hasn't even begun to work on.

But things are never easy. When NASA set out to put a man on the moon, they didn't start by loading a team of people onto their first rocket and launching it into space. Instead, they tested each piece of the technology through hundreds of incremental steps.

After DaVinci's time, we created many new areas of science and engineering so we could create many of the ideas he could only dream of. These included advancements in physics, material science, mechanical engineering, and modern-day project management.

The big accomplishments of the future will require an entirely new science, what I call "tool science."

So far we haven't had anyone step up to the plate and "declare ownership" of one of these areas. But flying drones on the other hand, are on the move — so to speak.

Communicating with the Future

Sometime over the coming months you can expect to see a version of the following help wanted ad:

> *"Help Wanted: Full-time aerial drone drivers needed to help manage our growing fleet of surveillance, delivery and communication drones. We are also looking for drone repair techs, drone dispatchers, and drone salesmen."*

With basic drone hardware being matched up with smart phones, and the bottom-up design capabilities of app developers around the world, drones will quickly move from the realm of personal toys to functional necessities that we interact with on a daily basis.

In 2010, the U.S. Military spent $4.5 billion on drones. This has been a rapidly growing budget item in the military's arsenal with $4.8 billion requested for 2011.

With this kind of focused spending, drone technology has improved dramatically over the past decade, but as a technology, the future for drones will go far beyond military uses. The stage is being set for thousands of everyday uses in business and industry all over the world.

AeroVironment Inc. recently introduced a life-size hummingbird-like drone, named Nano Hummingbird. The cute little device was funded by DARPA for possible military and non-military surveillance applications.

Google recently purchased a small fleet of micro-drones to help with its mapping projects.

At the 2011 Consumer Electronics Show in Las Vegas, Parrot unveiled a series of games that could be played with their iPhone-controlled AR Drones, sold in all Brookstone stores.

In preparation for London's 2012 Olympics, the UK is making plans to have a fleet of flying drones in place to monitor the crowds. But they are considering taking it one step further by equipping some of the drones with non-lethal weapons in case violence breaks out.

With military and police forces being the primary customers of drone technology so far, it's only natural that most of the industry's thinking has been skewed towards surveillance and weapon-carrying drones.

However, flying drones are an incredibly flexible platform for new technology to emerge. Simply adding elements like cameras, lights, audio, sensors or even a robotic arm can increase the utility of a drone exponentially. Here are a few unusual possibilities to help tweak your imagination:

- **Cruise Ship Drones**

    While the rest of the world has shifted from place-to-place to person-to-person communications, the cruise industry remains woefully behind. Cell phones and other handheld devices are not usable on ships without paying exorbitant connection fees. This can be solved with flying communication drones hovering above each ship. Since the airspace at sea is unregulated, this can be implemented with or without the approval of the cruise ship below. Doing some quick math, if 1,000 people were willing to pay $10 a day to stay connected, the income streams would be huge.

- **Communication Drones**

    Operating like communication satellites in space, flying communication drones will be a quick way to eliminate the shadows and dead spots common with today's tower-based cellular networks. The only things preventing more experimentation in this area have been legacy systems and the existing spectrum allocations that favor telecom incumbents such as AT&T and Verizon.

In a recent conversation I had with an executive in the aerospace industry, I was told that the entire country could be blanketed with high-speed wireless connectivity with a formation of 19 well-positioned communication drones hovering overhead.

- **Surveillance Drones**

Criminals fleeing the scene of a crime will have an entirely new set of police tracking devices to contend with when drones are brought into the mix. This may also be extended to border-crossing drones, prison-watching drones, and open-sea pirate and smuggler drones. Add a set of speakers to the drone, and an operator can start yelling at anyone engaged in vandalism, graffiti or littering.

- **Video Projector Drones**

Once a video projector is added to a flying drone, you suddenly have a marketer's dream tool with the ability to project images on the sides of buildings, on sidewalks, or even on the side of a moving vehicle.

- **Lighting Drones**

We've been trapped into thinking that lighting can only be managed from stationary positions, but that is about to change. Concerts and stage shows with flying spotlights or pyro-burst effects, TV sets, political speeches and opening night galas can all be enhanced when our lights start flying.

- **Strobe Drones**

High-intensity strobes can cause dizziness, disorientation and loss of balance, making it virtually impossible to run away. As a weapon to disrupt or disable crowds, this kind of technology added to a drone is just now becoming practical.

Flying strobe lighting on a movie set will open a different set of options, and floating concert strobes can create stage-show effects never before possible.

- **Audio Drones**

Drones outfitted with speakers are already being experimented with. Long Range Acoustic Devices (LRAD) are being used as loud hailers to emit warning signals, or when the volume is turned up, as weapons to deafen opposition forces with a jarring, discordant noise. Some ships now carry LRAD technology as an anti-pirate measure. As an example, LRADs were used to drive off pirates attacking the Seabourn Spirit near Somalia in 2005.

Audio drones, however, have far more potential in the marketing and entertainment fields. Floating and flying sounds create a far different sensation than stationary speakers.

Floating messages over nearby crowds may be the solution to draw attention to a mobile business, a time-sensitive special such as hot bread just pulled from the oven, or situational conditions such as announcing the sale of umbrellas during the start of a rainstorm.

- **Advertising Drones**

Planes towing advertising banners are a long-standing tradition for outdoor stadium events or wherever large crowds gather. But scaled smaller in size, with more maneuverability, drones towing banners or equipped with side displays for advertising are distinct possibilities.

- **Photography Drones**

The fine art of photography takes a new twist when flying camera drones become affordable. Photographers have long dreamed of being able to find the perfect angle for every shot, regardless of elevation or precariousness of the vantage point.

Going beyond the military's need to spy on people, photography drones are headed for more mainstream uses such as photojournalism, catalog photos, real estate photos, scientific research, slow-motion sequences and hobbyist experiments.

- **Gamer Drones**

Recently, Parrot introduced a number of games that could be played on their AR Drone quadricopters using an iPhone as the controller. This layout and design is setting the stage for many more smartphone-controlled drones with app developers providing a never-ending stream of new games.

For parents worried about their kids spending too much time playing games in their basement, the new concern will be about kids getting lost in the forest playing "drone wars."

- **Delivery Drones**

Thinking beyond traditional delivery systems, flying drones could be used to deliver food, packages or water, to change out the batteries in your home, to remove trash and sewage, and even to vacuum the leaves from your front lawn. For some people, the drones will allow them to live off the grid, and even off the net.

- **Robotic Arm Drones**

Add a robotic arm to a flying drone, and your mind begins to swirl with possibilities. A "flying arm" can be used as a probe in hazardous environments, a transport for dangerous chemicals, or a rescue mechanism for someone dangling off the side of a mountain.

- **Sensory Drones**

Many of today's drones have the ability to monitor air quality and map pollution flows. Future drones will have the ability to chart a wide variety of sensor-based data such as soil quality; moisture content; micro-temperature variations of air, land and sea; air densities; particulate matter; and the spread of plant diseases and micro-organism infestations.

- **Fireworks Dropping Drones**

When fireworks are manufactured, a large portion of the overall weight is dedicated to the propellant needed to launch the pyro-display into the sky. The propellant is also one of the least stable and least controllable components of the assembly. Fireworks designed specifically to be "dropped from the sky" would have far more stable characteristics and produce spectacular visuals for a fraction of the cost.

- **Search and Rescue Drones**

Very often, weather and visibility issues prevent a manned-rescue team from venturing into turbulent waters to attempt a rescue. For this reason, a number of unmanned rescue drones are being planned and tested to overcome our own "human" limitations.

- **Surveying Drones**

The process of surveying land and documenting the terrain can be greatly accelerated with the introduction of flying drones designed specifically for taking all of the measurements. Laser measurement systems coupled with topography mapping systems are a natural extension of current drone technology.

- **Weather Drones**

NOAA, the National Oceanic and Atmospheric Administration, had been testing the use of an Aerosonde Mark 3 drone aircraft to fly into the heart of hurricanes for more accurate storm predictions. In 2008, it was used to fly into Hurricane Noel but was purposely sacrificed to the turbulent winds of Noel as part of the process.

Next generation weather drones will be smaller, smarter, faster and more survivable to match the needs of virtually any research projects.

- **Micro Drones**

  Drones are getting smaller, and for some applications, nearly invisible. When drones begin to approach the nano-scale, traditional laws of physics begin to break down, and when flying in a nano-aircraft, air molecules are too far apart to provide consistent buoyancy. But as always, our current limitations create an excellent opportunity to uncover the true laws of "flight physics" when dealing with nano-particles.

While some science fiction writers have already speculated on the upside and downside of super tiny drones, the true potential is beyond our ability to imagine it.

With transportation becoming easier, making us a more mobile society, and with cell phones and the Internet speeding up our digital communications, our world is becoming a much more fluid environment.

Much like water that flows downhill using the path of least resistance, businesses and social structures have created a flowing set of decision points that move from areas that are less appealing to areas that are more appealing.

The future has needs, and it is our job to meet them. The good news is that we now have the ability to combine ideas far faster than ever before, but the tricky part now is to separate the good ideas from the bad ones.

That is why anticipatory analytics and trend analysis is so important. It also helps to get others as interested in the success of your vision as you are.

So how do you do that? "Incentivize" your vision.

Step 5: Incentivize Your Vision

"Beware of complexity disguised as solution."

One of the most famous lines in cinema history comes from "The Graduate." The character of Ben, played by Dustin Hoffman, receives a bit of advice from his father's friend. "Plastics," he tells the young man. "There's a great future in plastics." No truer words have ever been spoken.

Plastics have completely transformed the way the world operates. It's tough to think of any mass-produced object made without some type of plastic, whether in the form of technology, food storage, transportation or medicine.

And it all started with billiards. Love your iPhone? How about your disposable plastic fork, or the bumper of your car? Thank the Phelan and Collander Company, and thank a man by the name of John Wesley Hyatt.

You may not think much about the billiards industry. When you think about it, though, you quickly come to realize their ubiquitous

Step 5: Incentivize Your Vision

presence in bars, from roadside dollar-beer dives in the Mojave Desert, to high-end gaming establishments in Las Vegas, New York and Chicago.

Not that long ago, however, the very existence of this pastime was in danger of extinction. And it was due to the makeup of its own materials. If it had not been for the incentive put forward by one man in 1863, the game of pool would probably have never taken off in popularity. The reason for this would have been most likely tied to the extinction of the world's elephant population.

In 1863, ivory from elephants, walruses and hippo teeth, was the go-to material for lightweight durability in piano keys, buttons, ornamental hardware, and the like — essentially, everything that we would use plastic for now.

Following the industry trend of the mid-nineteenth century, every billiard ball used on every table around the world was made from elephant ivory. This placed the industry as one of the largest players in the ivory trade (I can only guess that piano makers were the only other manufacturers involved in such a scale).

There were some major drawbacks to the use of ivory in the manufacturing process.

First, no more than eight balls could be made from a single elephant's tusk, thus limiting supply for a sport quickly growing in popularity.

Second, the hunting of elephants very often killed the people doing the hunting. From what I've read, it's not easy to get ivory from an elephant. Many human lives were lost in the harvesting process. As much as we now lament the slaughter of elephants for ivory, that wasn't the top sentiment or concern in the mid-1800s. If something didn't change, the billiards industry was likely coming to an end.

Communicating with the Future

But one company, Phelan & Collander, a billiard and pool ball manufacturer, decided to change things. In 1869, they advertised a $10,000 prize for anyone who could find a proper substitute for ivory in the manufacturing of billiard balls. They didn't know how it was going to be done; they only realized that something, anything had to be done in order to do two things: break the industry free from a prohibitively expensive materials cost, and to stem the killings of human beings in the name of billiards.

Along came a man named John Wesley Hyatt, who saw a poster about the prize contest outside a bar in Albany, New York. Now, Hyatt was a resourceful man, and he had been trying to make his living as an inventor.

Soon thereafter, he came upon a sturdy, man-made substitute known as celluloid. It was a material that would revolutionize pool, enable the explosion of the motion picture industry, and eventually pave the way for the manufacturing of plastics, which arguably changed the world as we know it. All because of a simple prize contest.

When you get right down to it, the impetus for the Phelan & Collander prize stemmed from the recognition of mortality. Someone within the company realized that the sport of billiards could die, and along with it, the income generated through the manufacturing and sale of pool tables and cues.

In this case, the mortality of billiards was echoed in the very real mortality of the thousands of elephants and hundreds of humans who died on the savanna, in the attempt to harvest a product that had been previously thought of as inimitable. Once the decision makers really felt that clock ticking on the industry, they "ponied up" the money to make something happen. I guess time resonates with us only when we see a signpost of its end quickly rushing toward us.

So once you have fleshed out the concepts and details of your

80

vision, larger competitions can be staged to further incentivize the development of your concept.

THE NOBLE PURPOSE AND PEDIGREE

The most valuable incentive is that of the noble purpose. ✓

Going back to the Phelan-Collander prize that sought out a better billiard ball, that noble purpose was the saving of human lives for the sake of a game. It would be easy to think that the purpose was to save elephants, but the simple fact was that far too many people were dying in the harvesting of ivory.

The cost in human lives was far too extensive.

There was the need to solve a problem in an industry, but that problem was more important than the business of billiards — the prize creators wanted to lessen the mortal impact their business was having on the human population.

Today, websites like Innocentive.com connect solutions seekers and problem solvers to promote this type of innovation.

Furthermore, if a private company issues a prize for something that will help them personally, that's considered a very self-serving prize. They're missing the idea and impetus of the noble purpose behind it.

Somebody wins the prize put out by XYZ Company to solve an overheating problem that it might have in its boilers. I don't know what it might be. But that doesn't seem like it's worthy of a lot of people's efforts. Even though there might be a significant prize at the end, it would be a riskier prize and you wouldn't get the prestige, the same feeling of accomplishment as you would with something that has a noble purpose behind it.

I think it goes without saying that the goal of the prize competition itself must it be worthy of all the time and the effort necessary for the solution. For a prize to be truly "worth it," there must be an end point that people will respect and be willing to invest in.

This is the idea of the noble purpose. People have been gathering around what they perceive to be noble ideas for millennia, whether it's the siege of Troy, the Crusades, or the American or environmental revolutions.

In order for the vision to be fully realized, there needs to be a group effort. And people won't gather together in the manner I am suggesting, simply for the purpose of generating greater profits for you, Bill Gates, or anyone else — even if you're paying them.

Simple payment for the work of creative visionaries is not enough. Better results are gotten from individuals working together toward a noble goal — or an incredibly profitable goal, and if you're not able to guarantee that (who is?) then at least promise importance. Because this process requires full immersion in the subject; in order for it to work, the individuals must feel that the time and the effort are worth it.

So to accomplish that immersion, it makes sense for them to issue some sort of a payment along the way — incentives to drive things forward. The goal then, is to effectively choose some competing teams and to pay them (subsistence living at least) with milestone incentives to move things forward. Then, provide the team that actually accomplishes the ultimate goal a much bigger bonus at the end.

On the other hand, if you are working for something that's a noble purpose then the reward at the end is far less important.

It is important that the competition be noble, but it is also important that the pedigree of the prize-giver be weighty. The

British government can attract more quality minds than "Joe Blow's Big Prize." The use of these teams to accomplish a goal is known as "Crowdsourcing" as described in a very interesting *McKinsey Report* entitled "And the winner is…"

CROWDSOURCING

As of late, crowdsourcing has been a strong trend.

The idea here is that you can farm out your work, and people will work for practically nothing, engaging simply for the love of the game. I guess this can be effective or useful up to a point. But you don't really get the full depth of thinking that you need for a true creative revolution in your business.

Crowdsourcing, in my opinion, suffers from a 'mile-wide and an inch-deep' mentality. At some point, you're going to need full immersion from your talent. If you take your brightest and best idea junkies and give them the opportunity to become completely engaged in the process, the quality of output becomes far greater.

It's too easy to divert the attention of your best and brightest because, well, problems need to be solved in the daily operation. But believe me, this will only distract from the goal. There needs to be somebody, that visionary to lead the immersion effort — someone that is well-steeped in the topic and understands all its nuances. A team leader, if you will.

The Phelan & Collander prize mentioned above was not the first instance of crowdsourcing. There are other examples, such as the Longitude Prize of 1714, offered by the British government in order to find a way to determine the longitudinal position of ships at sea.

The winning device was known as the Marine Chronometer, which tracked elapsed time at Greenwich and was used to measure alignment of celestial bodies. For his work in this arena, a clockmaker named John Harrison netted the present-day equivalent of nearly $5 million for the advancements he made in the determination of longitude at sea. It would be no exaggeration to state that his influence on the colonization of America was enormous.

The interesting thing about this whole process is that it is dynamic. You don't just create a one-time vision and stick with it. There are lots of variations that happen along the way as new technologies come into play. As new political decisions, as new laws and regulations come into play. Things change, so these goals change, too.

Regardless, integral to the process of taking control of the future is the construction of a team. After all, it is the collaborative process that managers must rely upon to push their companies forward. Relying on a single individual is counterproductive, in that it places an unduly large load on one person, who will either get burned out or simply end up feeling like he or she alone feels responsible for all good, and bad, that comes out of the process.

I'm also a firm believer in the idea that the whole is greater than the sum of its collective parts.

And that's why I am proposing eight contests of my own — complete with noble purpose and global (team) involvement.

THE RACE TO THE CORE

People are at their best when they are challenged. If we don't challenge ourselves, nature has a way of giving us challenges anyway. There is great value in our struggles, and human nature has shown us that we value only the things we struggle to achieve.

Step 5: Incentivize Your Vision

That's why lottery winners have such messed up lives, because they haven't achieved anything. We are currently out of balance between backward-looking problem solving and forward-looking accomplishments.

In the challenges I propose, only countries will be allowed to compete — not companies, colleges or any other kind of organization. Each country will be allowed to submit up to two teams, similar in some respects to an Olympic competition. However, in these contests, there will be no second or third place. Teams will compete until one country wins.

At stake will be a combination of national pride, personal legacies and laying claim to unprecedented achievements in science and industry.

Behind this announcement is our team at the DaVinci Institute. To some, this announcement may be nothing more than an intellectual exercise to postulate eight grand challenges for the future. Our hope is that we may somehow stir the imagination of people around the world and, at a bare minimum, incite a global conversation.

The reason we have chosen eight competitions is because of the eight dimensions of the Octagonist as a competition framework. Very often the work that I do is in groupings of eight, and you are probably wondering what the significance is of the number eight. Have I always been tormented with an "eight" fetish? Is this some sort of obsession like Jim Carrey in the movie "The Number 23"? Will the world end if I somehow violate my own rules-of-eight?

The fact of the matter is that this is just a recent obsession, without any real origin and not really tied to any long-term strategy, at least not one that I can talk about in public. But rest assured, I am not eight feet tall, I don't have eight legs, and I don't have eight fingers. Wait, I'm sorry. I do have eight fingers, if I subtract the thumbs.

Communicating with the Future

But I did interview eight people last summer, listened to eight audio books, chewed exactly eight pieces of gum every hour, and celebrate "8:88 time" every day, which is actually 9:28 am and 9:28 pm. Does that make me someone who is just a few fries short of a happy meal? You'd say that only if you are one of those classic-four losers, a gambling seven-loving fool, or one of those weird "13 freaks."

For those of you normal people who regard this as a strange way of looking at the world, let me begin by giving you eight reasons why the number eight is so important.

1.) Eight is a dimensional number. It gives you all four directions above and a;; four directions below the horizon. When a three-dimensional graph is created with the X, Y, and Z-axis, it evenly divides the space into eight pieces.

2.) Eight is a power of two, being two cubed. Eight is the first cubed prime number.

3.) The number 8 is a Fibonacci number, being 3 plus 5. The next Fibonacci number is 13.

4.) Eight is the atomic number of oxygen, humankind's most important element.

5.) In liquid measurement (U.S. customary units), there are 8 fluid ounces in a cup, 8 pints in a gallon, 8 tablespoons in a gill, and 8 furlongs in a mile. Long live the furlongs.

6.) A "lazy eight" is the symbol for infinity. The classic Mobius Strip on steroids. Infinity is the opposite of nanotechnology, but then again, we still don't know if there is a limit to smallness.

7.) A polyhedron with eight faces is an octahedron, and for me a diamond-like object representing the 8 cylinder-like facets of an engine that will drive us into the future.

8.) I just happen to like the number eight.

If my reasons for working with the number eight still don't make sense to you, just get over it. Life seldom makes sense, and once we figure out all the things possible, the fact that I have an eccentric obsession with eight will be the least of your worries.

Let's begin looking at the future through this eight-sided lens.

Now, each of these eight competitions will be the most challenging ever imagined. Some may not be completed in our lifetime. They are designed to stretch human thinking and push the envelope of understanding.

Look at the first one as an example. The first competition will be a race to send the first probe all the way to the center of the Earth – 3,950 miles straight down.

LOOKING BACK AT THE EARTH'S CORE

In 1970, geologists in Russia launched into a major drilling project at the Kola Peninsula, near Finland, with the expressed intent to burrow into the Earth's core. After 22 years of working on the project, they had managed a hole the diameter of a small melon, extending 7.6 miles down.

The project ended when the crust turned mushy under the drill bit. They had bored into temperatures as high as 356 degrees Fahrenheit, much hotter than expected at that depth. The Kola

Peninsula borehole is by far the deepest hole ever dug, yet it stretched only 0.2 percent of the way to the core.

Today, the Earth's interior remains as frustratingly out of our grasp as it was 300 years ago when the famous astronomer Edmond Halley postulated that the inside was hollow and filled with living creatures. We consider his ideas humorous today, but the fact remains, when it comes to understanding the center of the Earth, no one knows anything for sure.

THE NEED FOR PRECISION

Geological textbooks describe the Earth in terms of four primary layers – the crust, the mantle, the outer core and the inner core.

The distance to the Earth core is roughly the same distance as between New York City and Stockholm, Sweden, or the distance between Warsaw, Poland and Calcutta, India. If we described the journey between these cities in terms of "four regions that you will go through," the description would seem at best, primitive.

We have no maps of the center of the Earth. We have no accurate diagrams, no understanding of motion, fluidity or changes happening with any degree of accuracy.

While scientists are developing skills to work with nano-scale precision on the Earth's surface, the best we can muster below the surface is blindfolded guesswork done with 100-mile precision.

What's happening below has a huge impact on what's happening above. Earthquakes, volcanoes, tsunamis and polar shifts are all happening because of changes happening below the surface.

As you can see from the chart below, many thousands of people die every year because of our own ignorance. Without any prediction systems, it's impossible to move people out of harm's way.

Number of Earthquakes Worldwide 2000-2010

Magnitude	2000	2001	2002	2003	2004	2005	2006	2007	2008	2009	2010
8.0 to 9.9	1	1	0	1	2	1	2	4	0	1	1
7.0 to 7.9	14	15	13	14	14	10	9	14	12	16	17
6.0 to 6.9	146	121	127	140	141	140	142	178	168	142	123
5.0 to 5.9	1344	1224	1201	1203	1515	1693	1712	2074	1768	1832	1313
4.0 to 4.9	8008	7991	8541	8462	10888	13917	12838	12078	12291	6852	6554
3.0 to 3.9	4827	6266	7068	7624	7932	9191	9990	9889	11735	2900	3052
2.0 to 2.9	3765	4164	6419	7727	6316	4636	4027	3597	3860	3009	2846
1.0 to 1.9	1026	944	1137	2506	1344	26	18	42	21	26	21
0.1 to 0.9	5	1	10	134	103	0	2	2	0	1	0
No Magnitude	3120	2807	2938	3608	2939	864	828	1807	1922	20	21
Total	22256	23534	27454	31419	31194	30478	29568	29685	31777	ⁿ 14799	ⁿ 13948
Estimated Deaths	231	21357	1685	33819	228802	88003	6605	712	88011	1787	226215

Source: USGS National Earthquake Information Center
ⁿ - As of Sept 13, 2010

THE GOAL

The goal of this competition is to develop a technology that can more easily probe the inner workings of the Earth, and do it with far greater precision.

The competition is not just about mitigating earthquake deaths, or knowing when the next volcano will erupt, or when the next shifting of the poles is about to occur. It's all that, and much, much more.

NEW TECHNOLOGY IS NEEDED

When it comes to the technology needed to get to the center of the Earth, that's where it gets fuzzy because some new kind of technology will need to be developed. At this point we can only speculate.

Geophysicists have built models of the Earth's core by studying seismic waves that ripple through the planet. Every year, thousands of earthquakes are recorded at the various seismic stations, with some intense enough to be recorded all the way through the Earth.

These waves flow through the Earth at differing speeds depending on the types of materials they flow through. The faster the waves, the denser the material. Seismological data is then overlaid onto our existing models of the Earth's interior to add more evidence about what lies below.

Everything we know about the Earth's core has been developed through indirect evidence.

Geophysicists, at best, can only describe the topography of the inner Earth with a resolution of many miles, not inches. So any probe traveling into the Earth will have to create its own maps along the way.

Some teams may consider using advanced boring technology. But that may not be the best approach when considering the distances involved. If an extremely fast boring technology enabled a probe to move at the blazing fast speed of one mile per day, it would still take nearly 11 years to reach the core.

Step 5: Incentivize Your Vision

One approach may be to use super thin nano-wires that worm their way along. Another may be to use high-powered lasers or some sort of plasma drill.

In addition to all of the other obstacles, two other challenges will be to find a power source capable of driving the probe, and developing a through-the-Earth communication system that works even through thousands of miles of molten rock.

COMPETITION REQUIREMENTS

The basic requirements for this competition are that the probe needs to begin on the surface of the Earth and travel all of the way to the center. As it moves along, it will need to communicate constantly, transmitting data to its team on the surface.

A series of sensors will be required for each probe. As the probe moves through the Earth, it will be required to create a data trail along the way.

The exact kind of data capture mechanisms to be placed on board the probe will be determined in the coming months. However, at minimum, it will need to be recording and transmitting the temperature, geo-location, pressure, radiation levels, consistency and makeup of the surrounding materials.

There will also be a requirement that the effort not cause irreparable harm to the Earth. We don't want to mess with the tectonic plates, interfere with magnetic fields, or inadvertently split the world in half. Undoubtedly some crazy ideas will be proposed. But in the end, this is an information-gathering exercise, not a win-at-any-cost competition.

WHO ARE THE TEAMS?

Only countries will be allowed to enter teams, and each country will be limited to no more than two teams.

There will be no limit to the number of people on a single team. That will be governed more by the county's own budget.

All teams will be required to maintain accurate records of their personnel, research data and stages of their development.

THE *PRIZE*

As in the Olympics, the winners will each receive a gold medal. However, the true value will come from the accomplishment itself.

In much the same way the Hubble Space Telescope has given us a never-ending stream of visual data about our universe, this technology will serve as a never-ending stream of discovery, mapping region after region of inner-earth geology.

For the material science industry, it will be a technology capable of locating deep Earth mineral deposits.

Most importantly, the team that wins will have carved out its own legacy with a permanent place in the history books.

ENTRANCE FEE

The cost of managing a competition of this scale will be significant. For this reason the entrance fee for each team has been set at $1 million USD per team. The money will be used to fund an endowment to ensure the long-term viability of this competition.

As the competition ramps up, an entirely new organization will be created. This organization will require a highly skilled management team and staffing with extraordinary technical expertise. This team will need to be in place for many years, perhaps even decades.

The amount also represents a tiny fraction of one percent of the amount each team will need to budget for their efforts. Team budgets will likely be in the billions of dollars.

GOVERNING BODY

Each competition will also require its own governing body. Since it will be a venture into the unknown, pushing the limits of science and technology, there will need to be an international governing body responsible for oversight and dealing with unforeseeable circumstances.

The exact makeup and responsibilities of this governing body will be determined over the coming months. But minimally it will include one representative per team from the countries they represent.

THE COST OF DOING NOTHING

The cost of doing nothing is far greater than the cost of doing something.

Communicating with the Future

Each year, billions of dollars are used to clean up after natural disasters occur, and much of that cost is being driven by our own lack of knowledge. Without any forewarning, we leave people in harm's way. Without understanding the scope of possibilities, our thinking is flawed, and our policies and planning are equally flawed.

Humanity has a higher calling than that of being habitual victims. Nature causes far more casualties than any war. If we are willing to fight wars, we should be willing to fight a war against cruelest monster of them all, our own planet.

The future is not being created by the meek and the timid. The future is being created by those willing to make bold moves, take on impossible challenges, and put themselves at risk. As I have said many times, there is great value in the struggle, and human nature has shown us that we value only the things we've had to struggle to achieve.

The future hates complacency, so much so that it has built-in self-sabotaging mechanisms to continually hold our feet to the fire. If we are not moving forward, we are instead moving backwards. There is no middle ground.

Humans are genetically hard-wired to compete. From early childhood we learn how to compete. We compete athletically in sports, academically in school, vocationally for our jobs and socially for our friends.

But we have very few of the grand challenges capable of moving humanity to a whole new level. For us to compete effectively, we need to know there's a finish line. And that's what we are hoping to provide.

In the end, this is a competition where all of humanity can end up a winner.

Step 5: Incentivize Your Vision

Whether you are solving the problems of the world or simply directing the future of your business, the act of controlling the future starts today — in the present.

Embrace the Future of Business

"Our visions of the future determine our actions today."

Ultimately, the best test for any futurist theory would lie in its future viability. How well does this "thing" hang around, after the passage of time and trends?

Because the future is an ever-changing, infinitely influenced system, I would say that any vision worth its mettle has the ability to accelerate, much like a car on a freeway entrance ramp. Your ability to accelerate your vision into the churning flow of ideas and trends is directly proportional to its success. Only the smallest of windows remain open for the most revolutionary of ideas in this ever-evolving world.

WHAT IS THE FUTURE OF BUSINESS?

The evolution of business has given rise to a new breed of worker. We are in the age of the perfection of the entrepreneur. Thirty years ago, we began to see the demise of the company man. Today, the creative professional is more likely to be an independent contractor, shuttling from project to project, filling the need for that individual, repeatedly called-upon, temporary influx of creativity that is no longer fostered in the corporate culture.

As a business culture, we have gone from the cultivation of talent in the farm system to the free-agency market where players are brought on for temporary gains and boosts in performance. Professional sports, a hefty attractor in its own right, has become a model for other creative businesses, providing a sex appeal and a market for those who embrace the pathos of the passion-driven Internet billionaire.

In fact, the average person that turns 30 years old in the U.S. today has worked 11 different jobs. In just 10 years, the average person who turns 30 will have worked 200-300 different projects.

Business is becoming very fluid in how it operates, and the driving force behind this liquefaction is a digital network that connects buyers with sellers faster and more efficiently than ever in the past.

But the effect of our flowing digital business world does not stop with how transactions are performed. Instead, it has begun to morph and change virtually every aspect of how business is conducted, including the duration and permanency of work assignments, the employer-employee relationship, and the organizing principals around which work assignments and talent coalesce.

At the heart of the coming work revolution will be a new kind of business structure serving as an organizational magnet for work projects and the free-agent talent needed to complete the work. This new structure is what I have conceptualized as a business colony.

BUSINESS COLONIES DEFINED

Business colonies are an evolving kind of organizational structure designed around matching talent with pending work projects. Similar in some respects to the craft guilds of the middle ages, colony operations will revolve around a combination of resident workers based in a physical facility and a non-resident virtual workforce. Some will forego the cost of the physical facility completely, opting instead to form around an entirely virtual communications structure.

Most will be organized around a topical area best suited for the talent base of the core team. As an example, a team of photonics engineers will attract projects best suited for that kind of talent. Likewise, a working group of programmers specializing in computer gaming applications will serve as a magnet for new gaming projects.

In some instances, large corporations will launch their own business colonies as a way to expand capability without adding to their headcount. Staffed with a few project managers, the company will use the colony as a proving ground for experimental assignments best performed outside of the cultural bounds of existing workflow.

Business colonies will develop their own standard operating procedures with consistent agreements, payment processes, legal structures, management software and methods for resolving disputes. Over time, they will be rated on their ability to complete tasks with specific ratings on efficiency, quality of work and how well they treat the talent.

THE DRIVING FORCES

The driving forces behind business colonies go beyond the fact that it is a good idea. Rather, colonies are being driven by a combination of technology, emerging culture and governmental systems that make it the logical next step in the evolution of work.

Businesses have an obligation to their owners and to their own workforce to hire the fewest number of people they can get by with. And while they have an obligation to treat their employees well, they have a competing obligation to not over-pay any of them.

Employment law in the U.S. is making it increasingly expensive to hire people. Each new-hire comes with the additional burden of managing benefits, payroll accounting, withholdings, human resource compliance and a wide assortment of other issues.

Every time a new "jobs" bill makes its way through Congress, any new decision points adds to the overall complexity of being an employer, and causes the burden of compliance to escalate.

As a result, companies are looking for ways to circumvent the escalating costs of adding staff, and project-based work becomes a logical option.

Additionally, technology is making it increasingly easy to match talent with waiting work assignments. Companies like Elance, RentACoder, Guru, and CrowdSpring are job-bidding sites designed to connect global talent with work assignments. However, even though they've built a solid base of operation, they tend to be a poor match for seasoned professionals who are not interested in competing on price.

SOMETIMES COLONIES MAKE SENSE, SOMETIMES THEY DON'T

Not all business situations lend themselves to a "colonized" workforce. Here are a few situations where business colonies are not a good fit.

- **Customer-Facing Jobs**

  Most customer-facing jobs such as retail sales and cashiers will probably not go away anytime soon.

- **Timing-Dependent Jobs**

  Timing-dependent jobs such as manufacturing, where one person's task is closely timed with the completion of another person's task, will not lend itself well to colony-based work.

- **High Institutional Knowledge Work**

  Any project that requires a deep understanding of a company's history, culture, and methodologies may also be a poor match.

- **Sensitive Issues and Trade Secret Work**

  Whenever a project involves proprietary information, sensitive issues, or a company's trade secrets, the work is best left in-house.

- **High Accountability Positions**

    Any position involving the handling of money, personnel records, or any senior management positions will require the work to be performed by loyal personnel.

While not every position will lend itself to the transformative nature of project work, managers around the world are about to embark upon a lengthy period of experimentation as they probe time and again to see what works and what doesn't.

THE PROJECT WORK LIFESTYLE

Given the choice between a stable 40-hour a week job and doing project work, why would anyone be interested in working on projects?

Indeed, there are many reasons.

Yes, some people may be unemployed and have no other options. But that scenario will play only a minor role, as most people running business colonies will be more inclined to work with those who are drawn to, and have acclimated to, the project-work lifestyle.

Young people today do not want to fall into the same trap that their parents were in, dependent upon a single employer with virtually no control over their own destiny.

Ironically, people who do project work today find great security in being able to bounce from one project to the next without having to quit or resign from the last position.

There is great freedom to be found in aligning yourself only with the projects well-suited for your interests and skills. In addition, the work becomes more meaningful and rewarding when someone is putting their reputation on the line and completing it in stellar fashion.

Even though the projects may come with strict deadlines, people also find greater purpose in being able to pick the projects they want, and in the flexibility to perform the work in a manner of their own choosing.

When you add up all of the positives – stability, flexibility, freedom, purpose, meaning and an ability to control your own destiny – the business colony lifestyle brings with it some powerfully compelling reasons to switch.

STRUCTURE

As a project flows into a colony, the first step will be to assess the overall size and scale of the assignment and break it into logical and chunk-able tasks. Some projects will come with fixed budgets, while others will determine the scope of work and negotiate the price as a preliminary step inside the colony.

Once tasks are defined and organized around a working timetable for completion, work projects will then be divided up and assigned to those who will complete them.

Most colony members will be business entities. In fact, many will require that all members form their own LLC or other type of legal entity for tax purposes.

One-person LLCs are the typical way for individuals to magically transform themselves into businesses and avoid tax accounting hassles.

Any payments will still be tagged as 1099 income, but direct payments to a company will eliminate tax filings, matching funds, and the complexities of payroll accounting. So the efficiency of any colony will hinge on the conversion of talent into private one-person business enterprises.

Even though each member of the business colony will be working as a business entity, project assignments will be based on the reputation of the individual.

REPUTATION MANAGEMENT

In a business colony environment, reputation is everything. People with stellar reputations among colony leaders will always be at the top of the call list whenever a new project arrives.

Those who come to a colony for the first time will attempt to work their way up the hiring ladder as a way of improving the odds of a project manager selecting them as they assign talent to each new project.

Some fast-moving projects may quickly expand outside of the bounds of a project manager's "friend network," and that is where referral systems and social networks come into play.

An online reputation consists of many things. Beyond the standard profiles and carefully crafted bios are an entire sub-layer of conversations, photos, videos, data sets and reference points that add to the overall impression someone will use to assess your abilities.

Similar to photo-stitching technology, which pieces together thousands of photos into one giant master photo, future reputation-stitching software will be used to develop reputation mosaics that sew together all of the online informational fragments into one comprehensive personality montage.

Thinking further, reputation-stitching software will incorporate various types of analytical tools for determining how well a particular project will match up with an individual's ability to perform on it. At the same time, other applications will be developed to help people optimize their reputations for working on certain types of projects.

THE EVOLUTION OF WORK SPACE

"Co-working" spaces, like The Vault that we operate at the DaVinci Institute, are the logical forerunners to business colonies. Most consist of an aggregation of talent with additional capacity to take on extra projects.

However, colonies will form in many different ways. Some will be private colonies run by large corporations. Others will form around a specific talent pool with specialties in such areas as metallurgy, bioinformatics, data mining, social mapping or video production. Still others will be nonprofit colonies formed around a specific cause like clean water, halting the spread of malaria or rebuilding Haiti.

Over time, colleges will begin to transform themselves into educational colonies with an assortment of internal business colonies designed to give students practical work experience that parallels their studies. Rather than tenured faculty, educational colonies will consist of "teaching entities" that are matched to curricula on a project-by-project basis.

DOING MORE FOR LESS

The business world is constantly being tasked with doing more for less. Virtually any company that cannot find ways to increase efficiency and reduce costs will not survive.

Typically the largest figure on a company balance sheet is the cost of labor.

Business colonies are an organic process of matching labor to projects for the exact duration of the contract. No more, no less. Overhead costs, compliance and accounting issues are all minimized to improve the overall efficiency of the operation.

I don't see business colonies as a way for corporations to take advantage of cheap labor, although many will try. Rather, the coming era of skill shortages will put talented people in the driver's seat with many commanding increasingly high rates for their unique abilities.

Over time, people will be credentialed by the colonies they are associated with. Each colony will carry a certain pedigree, and the earliest among them will become the Harvards and Yales of the colony world.

Communicating with the Future

In the future, few will be able to relate to the elaborate hiring and firing systems that we use today. As we enter the era of business colonies, business as we know it will become a thing of the past.

PUTTING IT INTO PRACTICE

Most companies operate within a paradigm of reaction. When bad (or good) things happen, they may or may not adjust their way of doing business. This reaction paradigm occurs, frankly, because it takes all they can muster to keep the doors open, make payroll and turn a profit.

It's a tough world out there, and the widely held belief is that we're all out there just trying to chip away at the world in order to make a buck. When things happen, you just do your best to hang on, and hopefully do better next time around. These are companies that are always preparing themselves for the last disaster.

Other companies plan for the future. They understand that markets shift, technology evolves and unexpected waves of mayhem occur. These companies do marginally better than the previous ones. They have resources to weather the storm.

Their leadership has given the murky future some thought ahead of time, and allocates resources to various strategies for adaptation to the ebb and flow of nature — they embrace it as the pattern that it has become and create new attractors and endpoints based on the present trends.

Great companies design the future.

Faced with this evolving reality, don't you think it would be best to understand, and even cultivate, this new working culture? As a futurist, I find it impossible to ignore the untapped potential currently amassing in coffee shops, co-working spaces, and live-work lofts around the world.

In the same way that economic factors in the Middle Ages and the Renaissance brought about the existence of the merchant and middle class, the world economy now fosters an environment where the freelancer must be respected. These unattached creative minds are making impacts in major corporations. The rise of this new worker-class should be recognized, respected and understood.

They are the "Futurati."

SO, WHO ARE THE FUTURATI?

Or better yet, who will be the Futurati? They are the culmination of several factors, a team comprised of different players, who operate in a manner outside the norm. And there are companies that have tapped into this revolutionary thinking. When we look to the success in innovation of Apple and Google, and the relative decline of IBM and Xerox, we find keys to the rise of the Futurati way of doing things. Now, I want to take this further. I believe we can put this lightning in a bottle in a highly repeatable and profitable way.

I propose that Futurati become a new job title in the coming years, something that can hold its own in the lexicon of 'engineer,' 'analyst,' 'programmer' and the like. These are thinkers and visionaries. And if we focus their talents, give weight to their potential, and organize our business structures around their abilities, we have the opportunity to do great things. All we have to do is recognize the connection between vision and reality.

Communicating with the Future

Every member of the Futurati will have gone through a personal awakening, and to them the work will be far more of a calling than a vocation — much like when Leeuwenhoek peered through his first microscope, or when NASA was able to get its first clear pictures from the Hubble Space Telescope, the Futurati experience will be massively transformative — and massively addictive.

Individual experiences will differ, but each will form a professional expertise around three distinct attributes:

1. Grasping for wisdom and understanding
2. Immersing fully in the task
3. Leaving the former life behind

TAKE FOR INSTANCE, THE TERABYTERS

Each morning Winston rolls out of bed, takes a quick shower, and begins to strap on the trademark Gargoyle gear. Named after the characters described in Neil Stephenson's "Snow Crash," Gargoyles are is people who equip themselves with a wearable computer of sorts, and who are constantly collecting visual and sensory data about their surroundings, while continually being jacked into the Metaverse (Internet). A Gargoyle streams the totality of his life experience. It's his job to do this.

Two years earlier, companies like Cisco began a campaign to promote the lifestyle of the Terabyter as a way to force the other industry players like AT&T and Verizon to step up their game. Within a few short weeks, seemingly everyone on the planet knew what the hottest new ultra-cool profession would be.

For Winston, his role in life is to serve as a human information node in the rapidly growing world of extreme data immersion. He is a human version of the spidering bots that tech companies currently use to scan the digital web. His income is both directly and indirectly dependent upon the amount of information he is able to amass on a daily basis.

Search technology companies, like Google, Yahoo and Microsoft, have agreed to buy the incoming data streams from Winston, and thousands more people like him, based on a percentage of ad sales associated with the display of his information.

The information Winston collects is being continually streamed to the server farms for search engines designed for the physical world. Each video stream coming from Winston is layered with object recognition software, geospatial coordinates and other sensory response data to the physical world around him into digital information that is searchable.

As full-fledged Terabyters, people can do whatever they want to — anytime, anyplace — and still make money. For a mere $5,000 worth of equipment, and a commitment to wear the gear relentlessly, virtually anyone can become a Terabyter, and the money will start rolling in.

Admittedly, this isn't a lifestyle that will appeal to everyone. The equipment is a hassle and the income is rather sparse to begin with. But those who stick with it will see their income grow and, over time, the equipment will become far less intrusive.

For people who start early and stick with it, however, this is the ultimate lifestyle. Every day is an adventure, finding new places to explore, new people to meet — never bound to a desk or a computer. Their livelihood is directly related to how active their lifestyle is.

The world of Winston is the world of the new worker-- a world of the Futurati, where value is assigned to a different kind of experience and earning power. In this world, the generation of information through experience is practically one with the earning of money. The information of pure experience is money.

CREATING A TERABYTER NETWORK

To be sure, there will be many players involved in developing a system to ramp up data collection to this level. All of the Internet service providers will have to gear up, new bandwidth needs to be allocated, routers and switching systems have to be changed out, browsers and operating systems will need to be updated, and search engine thinking will have to be revised.

Invariably, this whole shift will begin with a ragtag operation of sub-terabyters seeding the data universe. The initial capabilities will be quite limited, with regional test-beds set up to demonstrate the potential inside a single city. But once a major player like Cisco begins to smell an opportunity, everything changes quickly.

Terabyter gear is already available, but still in crude, marginally-usable formats. Video-capture goggles, helmets, and other devices will quickly morph into sleek, barely-visible equipment that can be mounted in, on and around the wearers.

Once the world gets a glimpse of the potential, along with the right incentives, Terabyter gear will begin to fly off the shelves, system registrations will skyrocket, and a whole new income-producing lifestyle will spring to life.

In addition to the ongoing video stream of a Terabyter's surroundings, the video images will be overlaid with biosensor response data, assigning emotional values to individual objects, places and people.

Each month, new sensors and data-collection gear will show up in the marketplace, and Terabyters will have to decide which elements to replace on their apparatus. Some of the initial dissension will stem from whether or not it's necessary to use humans. Terabyter equipment can easily be strapped onto cars and bicycles, but the most valuable data will come from the places that only humans could go.

To be sure, privacy and security issues will rise to the surface, but these will not be insurmountable matters.

BRIDGING THE RELATIONSHIP

After viewing the world through the lens of a Terabyter, I'd like to focus your attention again on the emerging relationship brewing between information and money.

Money based on rare commodities will hold its value until the commodity is no longer rare. Similarly, money based on confidence and trust will hold its value until faith in the system begins to dissipate.

For this reason, all money is fiat money, based on trust.

Money today is nothing more than information – digital nuggets that have been assigned value buried deep inside our information reserves. Mining for information is similar to mining for gold or any other precious metals. You have to know what you're looking for.

Currency has been the traditional system for transferring value in the past. In the future, our ability to manage and control information will enable many new systems for transferring value.

If you're still struggling with the concepts here, Dan Robles, founder of the Ingenesist Project, offers his predictions for 2020 based on "an entirely new form of capitalism whose velocity and voracity will take the world completely by surprise."

Hold on to your hats; the transition is right around the corner. And the change agents who will help usher in this new system will be none other than the Terabyters.

Communicate with Your Future

"The future is in control. "

For each of the Futurati, they will have their own story of having walked away from their former life to embark on their own personal adventure, an adventure filled with unknowns and far more questions than answers. Their friends will view them as obsessive, their families as having "lost it."

To the Futurati, however, the experience will be so revealing, so filled with possibilities, that nothing else will seem to matter.

As with the power of gravity, the future is an undeniable force drawing us forward. But the approach vector we're on can be changed, and it's up to us to change it. With gauges and dials appearing before our eyes, the control panels for the future are waiting for us to push the buttons, flip the switches and pull the levers. The driver's seat is screaming out for a driver, and no force of nature will deny them taking it.

As the speed of business accelerates in the coming years, executives will learn that it is no longer good enough to simply plan for the future. Instead, they will need to take ownership of it. To do this, they will need to employ those who understand how to stake a claim of ownership to a vision, and guide it to fruition.

In order to recognize the right candidate for this job, we should first look to the man whom I consider the godfather of the Futurati, literally, the very first Renaissance Man: Leonardo DaVinci. For me, he is the godfather of the Futurati and the model for two major components of this new intellectual class — a class with the potential to revolutionize the way businesses are run.

Our anticipations, hopes, and desires are all emitting powerful signals, and these signals can be channeled, directed and influenced. For those of us who feel our own mortality breathing down our necks and only a limited time to make an impact, it's easy to feel a great sense of urgency.

And this is why I believe that we shouldn't rely simply on planning well and awaiting the future. We should design it. We should engage and control that which is to come, at least in the foreseeable future, say three to five years out. After that, too much chaos invades the system.

Such is the task — to control the future, not to read tea leaves or gaze into crystal balls. The future is something to be engineered. It is a being to be constructed in the manner of a modern day Prometheus, to borrow the words of Mary Shelley. But it is not to be feared. And it is certainly not something we should be content just to 'let happen.'

This book is a call to action for those who understand the importance of seizing the moment, wherever and whenever it may exist.

In a recent conversation, a close friend of mine listened to my thoughts on this topic and asked me, "When it comes to controlling the future, how much control do we really have?"

To this I answered:

- "We can ignite the spark"
- "We can drive the vision"
- "We can cause the world to take notice"
- "We can implant new visions into the minds of the decision makers"
- "We can track the progress"
- "We can act on the results"

He then persisted, "No seriously! How much control do we really have?"

I concluded, "It's less than we want, but more than we think."

About the DaVinci Institute

"We are a community of revolutionary thinkers & innovators intent on unlocking our future, one idea, one invention, one business at a time."

The DaVinci Institute is a community of entrepreneurs and visionary thinkers intent on discovering future opportunities created when cutting edge technology meets the rapidly changing human world.

Based in Louisville, Colorado, the DaVinci Institute operates as a working laboratory for the future. The operation of the Institute involves a unique combination of coworking, educational and networking events, and special projects that percolate up from this talent-rich environment.

At a Glance:
- **Year Founded:** 1997
- **Business Form:** 501-c-3 Non-Profit
- **Total Staff:** 3 F/T, 12 P/T
- **Senior Fellows:** 14
- **Council of Luminaries:** 50+
- **Members of the DaVinci Institute:** Over 400
- **Total People Attending Events per Year:** Over 3,000
- **Total People Attending Futurist Thomas Frey Keynotes per Year:** Over 20,000
- **Total Website Visitors per Year:** Over 5 million

History of the Institute: The Institute was founded by Futurist Thomas Frey in 1997 in a small office in Longmont, Colorado. Since that time he has traveled the world many times making hundreds of key business contacts with internationally renowned experts. Since that time he has asked a number of these contacts to be part of the Institute's own mentoring network, the Council of Luminaries.

In 2010 the DaVinci Institute leased the former Valley Bank building in Louisville and established it as the headquarters for the organization. The facilities include office, meeting space, classroom, event room, conference room, and coworking space for the burgeoning population of startup businesses wishing to maximize their potential inside a community of serial entrepreneurs.

DaVinci Institute Websites: The Institute manages a rather large web footprint including the following sites:

- www.DaVinciInstitute.com – Primary website for the DaVinci Institute that focuses on all of the activities taking place throughout the organization
- www.FuturistSpeaker.com – FuturistSpeaker.com is dedicated to challenging your thinking, pushing your imagination, and creating the future.
- www.ImpactLab.net – The Impact Lab is a laboratory of the future human experience. This blog serves as a breaking news site for future trends and emerging technologies.
- www.DaVinciVault.com – Serves as the hub for all of the coworking activities at The Vault

Articles posted on DaVinci websites have a far-reaching effect with thousands of tweets, links, quotes and reprints every month.

Coworking - The Vault: Located inside the DaVinci Institute facilities is The Vault, a world class coworking space designed for telecommuting professionals, freelancers, consultants, entrepreneurs, revolutionary thinkers, small business owners. The Vault also serves a home base for a unique group of startups that the Institute is helping groom for success.

The Vault functions as a vibrant business colony for intensely bright people including web designers, executive coaches, software engineers, web developers, social media consultants/strategists, graphic designers, product designers, public relations specialists, inventors, entrepreneurs, and much more.

- Members of The Vault: 35+
- Website: www.davincivault.com

Events: The Institute produces a number of unique events ranging from the two monthly networking events - the Night with a Futurist and the Startup Junkie Underground - to a series of Boot Camps and Crash Courses primarily designed around serving the needs of businesses and entrepreneurs. Events feature a combination of talented thinkers and seasoned veterans who have fundamentally changed the business landscape. Our goal for each of these events is to serve as a turning point in the lives of all who attend.

- Number of Events per Year: 70-90
- Total People Attending Events per Year: Over 3,000

About the Author – Futurist Thomas Frey

"The greatest value in understanding the future comes from spotting the major cultural, demographic, societal, and economic shifts early and translating them into viable business strategies," says Tom.

As the Executive Director and Senior Futurist at the DaVinci Institute, Tom works closely with the Institute's Senior Fellows and Board of Visionaries to develop original research studies, which enables him to speak on unusual topics, translating trends into unique opportunities.

GOOGLE'S TOP RATED FUTURIST SPEAKER

As part of the celebrity speaking circuit, Tom continually pushes the envelope of understanding, headlining events with some of today's most recognizable figures: Tom Peters, Nobel Peace Prize winner Mohammad Yunus; former CEO of General Electric, Jack Welch; former New York City Mayor Rudy Giulliani; Former

President of Colombia, Andrés Pastrana; Prime Minister of Spain, Felipe González Márquez; Nobel Prize winning economist Joseph Stiglitz; Saudi Prince Turki Al-Faisal; and former World Bank President James Wolfensohn.

His keynote talks on futurist topics have captivated people ranging from high level government officials to executives in Fortune 500 companies including NASA, IBM, AT&T, GE, Hewlett-Packard, Pepsico, Frito Lay, Nokia, Lucent Technologies, First Data, Boeing, Capital One, Bell Canada, Visa, Ford Motor Company, Qwest, Allied Signal, Hunter Douglas, Direct TV, International Council of Shopping Centers, National Association of Federal Credit Unions, Times of India, Leaders in Dubai, HSM ExpoManagement, and many more.

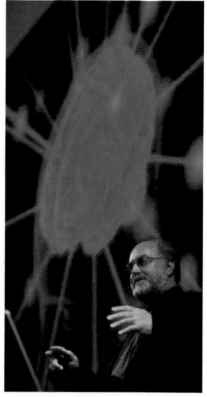

Because of his work inspiring inventors and other revolutionary thinkers, the Boulder Daily Camera has referred to him as the "Father of Invention". The Denver Post and Seattle Post Intelligencer have referred to him as the "Dean of Futurists".

Before launching the DaVinci Institute, Thomas spent 15 years at IBM as an engineer and designer where he received over 270 awards, more than any other IBM engineer. He is also a past member of the Triple Nine Society (High I.Q. society over 99.9 percentile).

Thomas has been featured in hundreds of articles for both national and international publications including New York Times,

Huffington Post, Times of India, USA Today, US News and World Report, The Futurist Magazine, Morning Calm (in-flight magazine for Korean Airlines), Skylife (in-flight magazine for Turkish Airlines), ColoradoBiz Magazine, Rocky Mountain News, and many more. He currently writes a weekly "Future Trend Report" newsletter and a weekly column on FuturistSpeaker.com.

CONTACT

DaVinci Institute
511 E South Boulder Road
Louisville, CO 80027

Futurist Thomas Frey
Senior Futurist at the DaVinci Institute
EMAIL: dr2tom@davinciinstitute.com
PHONE: 303-666-4133

Deb Frey
Speaking Agent
Vice President of the DaVinci Institute
EMAIL: deb@davinciinstitute.com
PHONE: 303-666-4133

Jan Wagner
Program Manager
EMAIL: jan@davinciinstitute.com
PHONE: 303-666-4133

"The future is in control. Isn't it about time you learned to communicate with it?" - - Futurist Thomas Frey